G AN

NARY

LIFE

International Coach Federation

Guest Name: _REMY_

References: Authors

⟶ Psy

⟶ Per........ying .... —

⟶ How to Influence People - Dale Carnegie

LIVING AN EXTRAORDINARY LIFE

Breakthrough Ideas from the
World's Premier Personal & Business Coaches

Lp

Lahaska Publishing
Buckingham, Pennsylvania

Living an Extraordinary Life

ISBN: 0-9650534-6-6
Library of Congress Control Number: 2001089883

Printed in the United States of America.

Lahaska Publishing
Post Office box 1147
Buckingham, PA 18912
www.lahaskapublishing.com

Table of Contents

Acknowledgements

I would like to express my heart filled thanks to everyone who has been part of this project, and to the entire coaching profession for the benefits they are providing to humanity.

There are several people whose efforts have made this book possible, specifically:

Terri Levine, my friend and co-publisher, for helping make this dream a reality.

Kim and Allen D'Angelo at Bookcovers.com, for their patience and creativity in the design of Living an Extraordinary Life.

Donna Eliassen, for her meticulous editing and dedication to excellence and for helping me to keep it all on track.

And of course, to all the authors represented here – you're truly the best!

How to Make $125,000 a Year
selling, Englewood Cliffs
N.J. Prentice Hall, Inc

~~16 steps~~

Erikson College

Columbia
(604) 879-5600

Teresa

Dear

I would like to
thank you for the
wonderful Xmas
Christmas
Party.

Your hard work
is highly appreciated.

Merry Christmas to you
and to your love one.
for Best wishes
for Best wishes New Year.
God bless you and your loved ones.

Sincerely,

Henry

Foreword

As a professional coach and the founder of Comprehensive Coaching U, The Professional's Coach Training Program, I have had the privilege and honor of getting to know the top coaches from around the world. Each one has their own unique gift, their own unique talent, and represents one of the many facets of what I believe it takes to live an extraordinary life.

I am excited to present to you the very best from the coaching profession. In this book are the very best people and concepts for creating a truly extraordinary life. I want you to take in the gems that each offers, try on those ideas (that might not feel comfortable to begin with), and expand your own extraordinary life.

As this book began to be born, I could hardly contain my joy in knowing that a collaboration of the very best material and ideas was going to be in one book, so that anyone who really wanted to achieve more, enjoy more, and experience life exactly as they choose to each and every day, would have the tools for personal excellence at their fingertips.

All of the authors are premier professionals whom I hold in high regard and I am thankful to them for their wisdom and their sharing.

Living an Extraordinary Life contains top coaching ideas and tips from leading coaches from the United States, Canada, and the United Kingdom. These are published here, in one place, so you can absorb them and create your own picture of your extraordinary life as you journey through each chapter.

My strong desire is that you will get exactly what you need to expand and manifest your personal excellence.

Enthusiastically yours,
Terri Levine, President Comprehensive Coaching U,
Inc. Author, *Work Yourself Happy*

Introduction

You are holding what is perhaps one of the most unique books you have ever seen. *Living an Extraordinary Life* is the combined effort of numerous people from across the globe. In the thirteen chapters that follow, you will be exposed to a wide variety of ideas, techniques, and experiences all designed to help you make your life truly extraordinary.

Each chapter is written by a different person and a few are written by several individual contributors. The authors, all top business and personal coaches, have shared with you their unique insights and experiences. Our aim is to provide you, the reader, with a variety of ideals and paths, which will help you in your life and career. You are free to pick and choose those chapters that appeal to you.

There is no right way to read this book. You may choose to read the chapters in order, or you may skip around, reading different view points at different times. I'd like to suggest you read the entire book, especially those chapters you feel are *not* for you. It is by stretching ourselves that we learn and grow.

Having worked with and been part of the team that produced *Living an Extraordinary Life,* I would like to express my gratitude and say that I feel privileged to have been acquainted with the authors presented here. When we began, I expected only to be publishing a book. What has happened is that I have enjoyed one of the most rewarding experiences of my life. The coaches represented here are among the most supportive and caring people I have ever had the pleasure to be associated with. Their dedication to helping people, and their concern for their fellow human beings is apparent throughout this book. My wish for you is that you have as much pleasure reading it and using the ideas presented here, as we have had bringing it to you.

Be well and may God bless you!
Jim Donovan, author, *Handbook to a Happier Life*

1

What is Life Coaching?

by Ewemade Orobator

Life Coaching is simply about removing obstacles from the *Coachee's* path that have restricted results in anything that is important to the Coachee. Having done that, via carefully considered and mutually agreed strategies, a plan of action emerges that takes the client to where they want to go. In short, coaching attempts to help people live the lives they have always dreamed of.

As a Life Coach, I focus on the benefits of coaching to maximize the attention and support given to the client. The hard work that could follow is put alongside clear pictures that I develop together with the client. In short, the pain to pleasure examples, which you may be familiar with, are used to motivate the client to achieve extraordinary results – permanently.

So what is the point of Life Coaching?

Jackie Onassis, more famously known as the First Lady when John F. Kennedy was US President, said that the greatest treasure in life was to find a purpose. Well, we all want a quality life – don't we! Surely, such a purpose does not have to be found, however, Dr. Philip McGraw[1] explains why, for many, there is this gap between an inherent purpose and fulfilment of the life we want to live:

> "You have always had within you every trait, tool, and characteristic necessary to create a quality life. What you did not have is awareness, know how, focus, and clarity." The purpose of coaching is to bridge the gap to a quality life.

What can Life Coaching really achieve ?

Simply put, the possibilities are endless. Life Coaching can truly help the individual to achieve anything that they truly wish to achieve and are seriously committed to achieve.

Here are just some examples:

- Life Coaching can help deepen and enhance one's ability to achieve the life they want.
- Life Coaching can help one to take oneself more seriously.
- Life Coaching can help one to find the resources to overcome personal blockages.
- Life Coaching can help one to explore and realise intrinsic goals.
- Life Coaching can help you achieve more health, wealth, and happiness than you ever thought possible.
- Life Coaching can help you achieve inner peace, develop the mind and an awareness of the spirituality that is in us all.
- Life Coaching can help strengthen one's most valued relationships.
- Life Coaching can help one live a life consistent with one's own values.
- Life Coaching can help maximise the opportunities presented by decisions and life transitions.

Is it possible to have more powerful purposes than the above?

Throughout this book, you will discover how ordinary people have helped other ordinary people, as well as themselves, to pursue excellence. Use this book to join the growing army of achievers who, like you, want even more success than they have already. Join them in pursuing personal excellence based around universal core values.

Life Coaching strikes at the very heart of life - to find a purpose or a mission that makes it worthwhile getting out of bed in the morning. Thus coaching is the vehicle that makes the journey, which one decides to go along, safer and more certain to reach its latest destination.

For this purpose to be achieved, a Life Coach must help the Coachee set powerful goals, for which the Coachee takes responsibility, and commit to maximizing the best options that they are aware are open to them.

What methods do Life Coaches use?

Many people have asked me about the methodology of Life Coaches. There is no rocket science involved in coaching. It is not personal development by a different name either.

Life Coaches use a variety of focused support techniques that are thorough and easily understood at either the simplest level or the most sophisticated level. The client is helped in every way to improve his or her performance. These support techniques address common faults and offer concentration on the focal points of each skill.

This support can be given over the telephone, face to face, over the Internet, or at group forums, events, and seminars.

Motivational speakers are known for giving "the path to success" as a proven tool kit that works. Some organizations, like the Life Coaching Academy, favour exploring options and the commitment of the client in determining the answers from within. There is no wrong or right approach, and the saying of "different strokes for different folks" is quite true.

What Coaching is not

Life Coaching is not a Science, which is, amongst other characteristics, a systematic knowledge of natural or physical phenomena, or the ordered arrangement of facts under classes, heads, or laws.

Life Coaching is not a Crutch. Coaching is a philosophy and not a tool to be used "as and when". It is a commitment to continued self-development and improvement and should not be dependent on any Coach.

Life Coaching is not a Fad: Buzz words come and go – as do fashions. There are those who believe that Life Coaching is such a fad. But as the UK College of Life Coaching can testify,[2] hundreds, including from every area of Europe, are now expressing an interest in life coaching. I also know that the International Coaching Federation has doubled its membership to over 3,000 in the last 12 months. Thousands of people have already benefited from life coaching. And it is not only the individual, but also large companies who now realise that performance is maximized when potential is maximized and when self-esteem and self-belief is at its highest level in the individual.

Life Coaching is not a Panacea. Despite the ageless relevance of coaching, it would be unhelpful and grossly misleading to suggest it is the answer to all cases of under-performance or no performance. Yes, behaviour can be developed to maximise the chances of desired results, but sometimes the entity might be broken and cannot be fixed. A leaking pot will not be fixed by the Coach and Coachee seeking to maximise its performance. Sometimes a new kettle is needed. Using the SMART Framework, a useful coaching tool: Specific, Measurable, Achievable, Realistic and Timed goal(s) can be set.

Why Life Coaching is not counselling

Life Coaching has been called "counselling by another name". It would be churlish not to recognize that there are a few similar characteristics between coaching and counselling. However, Life coaching is not counselling.

Coaching, like counselling, is a listening skill where one seeks to ascertain relevant information in a non-judgemental manner. It is a one-to-one, no obligation relationship with clear terms of reference.

It is the starting point of help that is needed, which distinguishes whether a Coach or Counsellor is needed. In other words, it is dealing with the baggage that may be present and stopping someone from moving forward. The Coach can only assist when this baggage (normally physical and/or emotional trauma) is dealt with first. If it is still there, the Coach needs to recommend a Counsellor.

Why Life Coaching is not psychoanalysis

Psychoanalysis starts from further back, from an even deeper starting point. If you were to imagine a line from left to right with 1 being the starting point where counselling is needed, and 10 being the end where coaching can begin, psychoanalysis would start at minus 5. This is because where counselling begins, a clear problem exists that needs dealing with. With psychoanalysis, a serious malfunction is present.

To understand how to deal with this malfunction requires a recognition that the malfunction would have been fed by unconscious behaviour of which the client does not appear to be in control. These factors may be impulses, wishes, or fears that each person has, without realizing it. The objective of Psychoanalysis is to reach the unconscious, revealing the conflicts which are ingrained in the patient's mind.

Why Life Coaching is not therapy

In the case of therapy, there are clear elements similar to psychoanalysis. There is a need to look back in order to move forward, and it is viewed as an appropriate treatment when some sort of mental order has been lost, no matter how temporary. That is why therapy is useful for momentary dysfunction such as mental breakdown.

However, there are clear distinctions to be made between therapy and coaching. Specifically, these are about allowing the space for healing, for in-depth understanding, and reconciliation with issues from the past that could threaten real achievement and enjoyment now and into the future.

Life coaching strategies for a better way of life

So, how do Life Coaches go about specifically helping to bring measurable and lasting positive change to peoples' lives? Well, let's look at some briefly to give you an idea.

Relationships: One of our most fundamental needs is to feel appreciated and feel wanted. Via life coaching, specific elements in one's strategy would include help on finding a relationship, asking for what you really want, deepening existing or new relationships, increasing self awareness in relationships, coming to terms with relationships that have ended, and widening one's circle of friends.

Money: Of course money cannot buy love, but it is needed in a capitalist society, and people do strive for more of it.

So a specific strategy would centre around increasing income, cutting expenses, planning and managing a budget, developing a financial plan and savings plan, a living expenses account, and retirement planning.

Time Management: One of the greatest, yet underestimated, resources – effective use of time – is a key area that life coaching can address. Thus a specific strategy here would include: a plan to get organized by removing personal and systematic clutters, a prioritization strategy, identifying what is important to you and not being distracted by seemingly urgent things, giving more time for you, and measuring progress.

Health and leisure: All of us want to be as healthy as possible and enjoy our leisure time. So making this happen is another area that life coaching can address. A strategy would cover: a fitness and diet programme that is fun and easy to follow, development of a motivational maintenance system, identification of support resources, and ensure that a disciplined approach is agreed to.

Personal Development: The world changes; so do we, and so must we. Life coaching can address this by changing the way we see ourselves; maximising the power of the mind; putting goal building steps in place; offering specific learning techniques, including the ability to learn faster; and encouraging a commitment to continuous improvement so that we do not stop growing.

Finding a purpose: All the above is possible, if you are clear about what is important to you. If not, as unfortunately, most people are not, then life coaching can fill this gap. Specifically this means help in: establishing core values, identifying what you enjoy doing, noting your personal skills (not just formal qualifications), noting your network, putting a capital F in fun, helping you to feel peaceful whenever you want, and identifying things or people holding you back.

In summary, a Life Coach will help you to identify whatever is important to you and put control back into your life. The measurement of our success is that stress is managed in your life, you have designed the life that you want, and that second best is no longer an option to you.

What makes for good Coaching?

Making the client look good and feel great is what makes for good coaching. This means the clients feel in control, they have a renewed or clearer focus of purpose, confidence and self esteem is in abundance, they have a lasting zest for life, and a desire to explore new opportunities. For me, there are a number of Success Factors that make for excellent coaching:

Success Factor No. 1 – Full Listening: Whether coaching is carried out over the phone or in person, listening is the number one factor, above all else, to ensure the foundations for a quality coaching session. According to a major survey[3], when we speak only 7% of what we take in is from the words we use, whereas 55% is body language, and 38% is our tone of voice. This means that over the phone, the majority of our communication method cannot be picked up. How this is rectified is covered in success factor No. 2 below. However, even in person, this research shows that relying on what is verbally said will lead a Coach hopelessly astray. So we must use our eyes to listen (55% Body language) to most of what is being said.

But listening involves more than that. A good Coach already knows that they should not pre-judge or filter the information given, and seek to listen.

As Stephen Covey[4] has stated, "active listening is based on seeking to understand first before being understood." So this means every time Coaches agree or disagree with a comment made, they are filtering or making a judgement. That is not active listening. Every time Coaches offer advice, they are likely to be recalling their own experience, which has nothing to do with the Coachee's experience. Every time Coaches evaluate what is being said, they are weighing up the information and coming to a view based on their own values and experiences, and not the Coachee's. And finally, every time Coaches probe and ask questions of the Coachee, they are framing the response, and thus getting the Coachee to talk about what the Coaches want to discuss and at their pace, rather than the Coachee's.

Success Factor No. 2 – Effective Questioning: This is not to say that the Coach cannot ask questions. Indeed, effective questioning is another hallmark of a good coaching session. The skill is to ensure that the questions asked are *assertive* rather than *insertive*. The latter takes up the Coachee's space and takes away their control, whereas effective questions can help restore focus to blurriness, precision to lack of direction, and decisiveness in place of uncertainty.

Success Factor No. 3 – Mutually Shared Values: What I am referring to here has nothing to do with the Coach and Coachee liking similar things or holding the same personal beliefs or priorities. This is about ensuring both parties can work together on the basis of trust and mutual respect. The experience should add value to both parties' lives. This means that both parties must trust each other and commit to work openly and honestly with each other.

Success Factor No. 4 – Plan of Action: Walt Disney once said that a dream remains a dream until you write it down, and then it becomes a Plan. The good Coach, having agreed to a plan, should write it down, ensure that the Coachee has written it down, and just as important, ensure a shared meaning exists as to what is meant by each aspect of the plan.

Success Factor No. 5 – Progress & Review: Having agreed to a plan, systems should be built into the relationship to have regular reviews on top of the call by call or session by session review. These will facilitate decisions being made as to strengthening what is working, and making honest decisions about what is not working. Systematic reviews will help identify any failing owing to lack of performance or lack of success that could be reversed by persistence. Whatever the case, the good Coach would not allow the Progress Review meetings to be anything but a positive learning experience from which the Coachee emerges feeling even more refreshed and focused on the goals.

Success Factor No. 6 – Success Management Plan and/or Setback Strategy: The good Coach knows that success comes in stages and supports the client in recognizing this, and celebrates achievements when they come, as they will. Of course, this does not mean praising each and every task completed, however, it does mean deliberately taking stock of things as they progress and celebrating success at suitable intervals. The Coach should ask, (as one of their standard effective questions), "What have you done today to celebrate what you have achieved so far?"

Equally, the good Coach will recognize that progress is not necessarily a straight road and that it will not be all glamour and glitter. If they are doing their job correctly, they will have prepared their clients for setbacks. This would involve identifying possible icebergs and what to do if they strike. The strategy would also involve allowing space for the Coachee to take stock of the setback, maybe pause (not quit), and start again when refreshed, and if relevant, be better prepared for the task ahead.

If each of the above success factors is properly deployed regularly, effective coaching sessions will occur as naturally as breathing. These are an unbeatable set of success factors, and the stakeholders can deploy them certain of their destination.

Life Coaching: Meeting the challenge of the new age

Life Coaching is meeting the challenges of the *new age*. People want results quickly, simply, to be lasting, at their convenience, on demand, and cost effective. They want more, they want to grow, and it's got to be fun getting there.

Life Coaches stay with the client to help implement the new skills, changes, and goals to make sure they really happen.

Clients with Life Coaches find that:

- [They are taking themselves and their hopes more seriously.]
- [They take more effective and focused actions immediately.]
- [They stop putting up with what is dragging them down]
- [They have created momentum so it's easier to get results.]
- [They have set better goals.] *ranch* *: children University*
big farm *graduate*
own business - specialty secret
garden
Life Coaches, like myself, always centre around the following *serenity,* objectives: *peace°*
quiet
solitary

- [Strengthening the client's Personal Foundation.]
- [Helping the client beef up their reserve and stamina to succeed.]
- [Helping the client set goals based on their Personal Values.]

By including these with what their clients want, Coaches help their clients have fun as well as enjoy regaining control of their lives.]

Life Coaching works because:

- The synergy between the Coach and Coachee/client creates momentum.
- Better goals are set - ones that naturally *pull* the client towards the goal, rather than require the client to *push* themselves towards the goal.
- The client develops new skills, and these skills translate into more success.

Coaching is becoming so popular because it is meeting the challenge of the New Age:

- Many people are tired of doing what they "should" do and are ready to do something special and meaningful for the rest of their lives. Problem is, many can't see it,

11

or if they can, they can't see a way to reorient their life around it. A Coach can help them do both.

- People are realizing how simple it can be to accomplish something that several years ago might have felt out of reach, or like a pipe dream. A Coach is not a miracle worker, but a Coach does have a large tool kit to help the big idea become a reality. (Fortunately, people now have the time and resources to invest in themselves and in this kind of growth.)

Live the Life you have dreamed about

It was so refreshing to be a Guest Speaker at a local Middle School and asking the 10-11 year olds whether or not they had a dream. All of them said yes, and many shared their dreams with me. What was even more uplifting was that every one of the 80 children in the room raised their hands instantly when I asked if they believed that they would achieve their dreams.

Our mission as Coaches is to restore that belief in the adult which is there in abundance in the child. It is possible if the desire and self-belief are there. The client comes to us with the desire and leaves us with the self-belief, awareness, and willingness to act and take responsibility to ensure they live the life they used to dream about. A Coach helps their clients to win again.

Most people believe that "hard work and doing it on your own" are the keys to finding the life, success, money, or happiness that they seek. They believe that a price must be paid to attain what they want, and often that price is poor health, not having enough time to enjoy life, strained family relationships, or lessened productivity. The saddest part is that even though this effort may result in more of something, it is often not the something they had in mind, and they are back where they started, or worse, further from their real intentions. The joy of coaching is to end this myth and help deliver the greatest gift of all - the opportunity to serve. For all of us as Coaches, it is an honour and a privilege to be offered such an opportunity.

Enjoy Life Coaching with your clients, and if you are not a Life Coach, I trust I have shown you how Life Coaching can and does help thousands of people to live the life they have always dreamed of.

About Ewemade Orobator

Ewemade Orobator, 37, is a qualified Life Coach who has been coaching since the age of 17. Qualified via Life Coaching Academy, he is also a member of the United Kingdom College of Coaching (UKCLC) and the International Coaching Federation and a Licensed Neuro Linguistic Programmer (NLP), having been personally trained by NLP founder, Richard Bandler.

In five years, he built his business from literally £1 to one that has now turned over £5m.

He has trained and supported clients from the second biggest law firm in the world, to a leading investment broker, and a professional footballer. One of his biggest projects involved supporting over 1,800 clients within a £100m investment scheme.

He has published written and video material in 2000 and 2001 and has addressed, as a guest speaker, over 40 local businesses, social clubs and schools in England. He also runs seminars including the highly acclaimed "How to build a £1m business from only £1".

Ewemade is married to his wonderful wife, Anna, and has a beautiful daughter, Carmen. He is a keen sportsman, playing Cricket, Soccer, and Tennis to a high standard.

Ewemade believes the greatest influences on his life to date are his mother, his wife, his friends, and all those who have believed in him and given him the opportunity to repay their faith and friendship. *Thank you.*

Visit his company's website at:

www.powerpsyche.com

Bibliography

Covey, SR. *7 Habits of Highly Effective People*.
Robbins, A. *Awaken the Giant Within*.
McGraw, Dr. PC. *Life Strategies*.
Torrington, D., and J. Weightman. *Action Management: The Essentials*.
Whitmore, J. *Coaching for Performance*.

[1] Life Strategies: Stop Making Excuses, Vermilion
[2] http://www.ukclc.net
[3] Figures taken from Gerard Egan's Skilled Helper
[4] Covey SR, Op Cit

2

Eighteen Steps to a Balanced Life -
Reclaiming Your Natural Energy

By Robert A. Arthurs

GOAL SETTING

Everyone tells you that you must have goals. The power of goal setting can never be underestimated, but the goals you do set have to be realistic. To create a balanced life, we have to have goals for each of the areas that make up our existence: spirituality, relationships, health, personal growth, prosperity, and community. For each of these areas of our core being, we should set three or more goals. Write them down and review them as many times as you wish; rearrange them every six months if they are unrealistic, then review and adjust them again. If you are self-employed, be sure your personal goals are aligned with your business goals. Also, share your dreams and aspirations with someone close, so if things get rough, they can gently remind you and help you get back on track. To achieve your goals you need your natural energy, and there are many robbers of this precious commodity. And if you really want to stay focused, hire a Coach!

grapple - struggle to deal
         or understand

Commitments

Keeping commitments takes a lot of discipline. People may have the greatest of intentions, but following through is the problem. In my 17 years of self-employment, I have come across many individuals, including some among my own employees and my Coaching clients, who have very low self-esteem, and who grapple with the concept of commitment. If you're one of these people who break commitments, I have news for you – you are not alone. It's a worldwide problem, and what it's costing you is a major loss of energy. Every commitment that you break, a strand of energy comes out of the top of your head affixed to that commitment, and another strand of energy attaches itself to the object or person with whom you broke the commitment - I know people whose hair looks like they put their finger in a light socket!

Completing your incompletes

Completing your *incompletes* takes as much discipline as keeping commitments. The impact of incompletes will not only rob you of energy, it will give you a feeling of failure until it is put away or finished. Remember that diet you started with great intentions, on January 1st? It only lasted a few months, and the formulas are still on the kitchen counter staring you in the face as if to say, "Failure! Failure!" Throw it out, or try again. Do anything; just don't leave it sitting there, robbing your energy. You know those books still lying beside your bed that you intended to read? Great intentions again, but don't just feel badly that you have not read them, especially the one covered in dust, with the bookmark inserted half way through; take the bookmark out and reschedule it for another time. Put away all unfinished, unopened books and breathe deep - you're free!

Connect with your higher power

Spend a few minutes each day in quiet prayer or meditation. Study after study shows that spiritual people live longer and cope better with stress. In terms of how you cope, whether it's meditation, prayer, or going to church, it seems to have a positive effect. Studies found depressed patients who practiced their own form of spirituality coped better than a control group.

Exercise your brain and have a yearning for knowledge

Exercise your brain, as you do with your body, with many tough exercises and provocative thoughts. Just as your muscles need stretching, so does your brain; commit yourself to doing personal development, hire a coach, read a good book, and create a zest for knowledge. (Or if you're like me, you'll go around with a supply of tapes.) Higher levels of education have been linked to better health, decreased risk of Alzheimer's disease, and increased survival rates following heart attacks. Heart doctors involved in an international study, which examined a correlation between higher learning and heart attack survival, suspect that education helps patients to understand disease, thereby giving them a weapon with which to combat it. So, hit the books!

Start an exercise program

Hire a personal trainer to push you. A personal trainer will determine your limits and what you are capable of, and will put you on a program of accelerated fitness. Exercise programs are one of the fastest ways to improve your self-esteem and get you feeling good about yourself. A good personal trainer will also advise you on your body type and what the best foods are for you to eat. So, get out there and take Rover for a walk. You might enjoy it more than he will! And besides being great exercise companions, pets are known to reduce the blood pressure levels of their human owners.

Do not sweat the small stuff

Quit sweating the small stuff; stress will rob your body of energy. Enrol in sport or exercise classes, like Tai Chi, yoga, or martial arts. If you think you are suffering from depression, seek medical attention or counselling, in addition to taking up some form of physical exercise. Perhaps you may have to consider some form of medication. Whichever options you choose, do try to include at least seven hours of sleep per night.

Telling the truth

Someone told me once that if you told the truth about everything, you would never again need to remember things from yesterday. The Bible also tells us that the truth will set us free. Telling the truth is part of keeping your commitments. Don't you want to be free?

You are what you eat AND drink

How much water do you drink daily? Are you eating enough water based foods, such as sprouts, melons, grapes, etc? Water allows the body's processes to function smoothly and prevents dehydration. Without adequate water, our bodies become less sensitive to thirst, so we are more likely to confuse thirst with hunger signals and then overeat. Choose mineral water for an added calcium bonus: as much as 50 milligrams in a 250 millilitre serving, depending on the brand. And always eat right to booster energy.

Drink more water; thirst is often mistaken for hunger cravings. Research has shown that a chronically dehydrated state makes us sluggish. Eat less sugar; too much sugar makes our insulin levels skyrocket, sending a message to the body to stop metabolizing fat. Reduce your fat intake and watch what kinds of fats you do eat, because some fats are "healthier" than others i.e., nuts, olive oil, avocados, etc.

You should aim to eat smaller, more frequent meals, including fruits, vegetables, and grains, and if you must snack, choose a healthy snack like a muesli bar instead of a chocolate bar.

Clean out your closet AND spaces

Going through your closet is a good metaphor for reviewing your life. You've had great intentions to wear some outfits that have been sitting in the closet for six months or more, but if you can't remember the last time you wore something, give it away! Do you remember when you bought that outfit for Sylvia's party two years ago, and you have not worn it since? Give it away!

Recently, my wife gave away a pair of jeans that I had custom made for me in the late 80's. I was shocked by the realization that I had kept those pants for 12 years, yet had only worn them six times. But they were "cool", and were a 29 waist. I am now a 33-34 waist! But you know, she actually did me a favour. Every time I saw those pants, I remembered the "good ole days" and felt an instant energy drain (youth, wild times, going days without sleep, etc.) No matter how much I exercise now, the best I could probably slim down to, or even want to be, is a 30-31 waist. Best to get rid of the jeans and move on. You must do the same, and if you think you can't do it, ask a friend who has no attachment to your clothes. You can also use this exercise to clean up the clutter in your home or your office.

Take control of your credit and finances

Give yourself a financial check up! First call your local credit bureaus and ask them to send you a copy of your credit report. This report is what the lenders review to determine if you are credit worthy. Not all credit bureaus report the same things, so cover your bases and call all of them in your area. If you find something that is incorrect, or that you are disputing, have the credit bureau add your side of the story to the report. And if it's just plain wrong, have the bureau remove it.

Create an Asset list; go through your house and list everything of value. Nine times out of ten you may find you own a lot more than you thought, in which case, it's time you upgraded your insurance content policy. This asset list is surprisingly effective as a small business balance sheet; a useful tool, as many companies start up with the owners doing the books themselves and learning as they go. Many buy small tools and equipment and expense it, but never add it to the asset side of the balance sheet. My own company found $57,000 worth of assets in the three years that we expensed, but never depreciated.

Eliminate duplicate insurance policies; do you know what kind of Life insurance you have? Do you pay the appropriate Tax? How's your bookkeeping knowledge? If there are any areas in which you lack expertise, just remember that it's *your* finances, or there will be someone else who has the keys to *your* dream.

Be a carer and a sharer

Feed your heart; be a volunteer. Do you ever wonder why some people who seem to have it all are so miserable, yet others who likewise seem to have it all are very happy? Chances are that the ones who are very happy are involved in their community in some shape or form. Community work has been known to make volunteers, as well as others involved, feel good. We are all searching for fulfillment, and of all the people I have met, the volunteers in the community have always been the most joyous. No matter what higher power or religion you believe in, these higher powers call us to help one another, especially those less fortunate than ourselves. Even if you can't offer financial assistance, you can still offer your time. Many people give money but will not give time, and a lot of people in the community actually need the time offered by the physical assistance of volunteers, more so than money.

Stay away from overwhelm

One main cause of people getting into an overwhelmed state is their own disorganized habits. Are you like most people who have a lot of clutter, or do you like clean surfaces? Being overwhelmed starts with our procrastination to clean up. Many organized professionals will tell you that if you have a problem with organizing your habits, rather than changing the ones you have, simply enhance them. What they mean is if you drop your coat by the door everyday, you should have a hook by the door to hang it on; if you drop your small change on the middle of the dresser, you should have a container there to catch it; if your telephone message centre has papers strewn all over it, you should have a tray there to contain it. Do you get the picture?

Watch your "self talk"

Do you talk to yourself out loud, or do you talk to yourself internally? Either way, we all do it. Do you blame everything that goes wrong on someone or something else? It's what we say to ourselves that counts. We have 60,000 thoughts a day, 95 percent of which are thoughts of yesterday. Also, 95 percent of the population strives for mediocrity, and only 5 percent strives for excellence. Many of us are still living with past memories of the *good old days*, rather than thinking of today and the future. We should be thinking and talking to ourselves in terms of the *good new days* which lie ahead. Many of today's top executives keep pace with the future in their thoughts, developing strategies that enable them to anticipate their competitor's next move and stay ahead. So take note the next time you are talking to yourself. Are your thoughts self-defeating, or are they self-motivating? We do have a choice, and it's what we choose that gives us the energy.

Create or maintain meaningful relationships

What good is success if you cannot share love, celebration, promotions, etc., with others who you care for? Do you go into relationships to take? Or do you go into relationships to give? If you go into a relationship to give, you will receive that same treatment back tenfold. If you want respect, give respect. If you want to be loved, give love, etc. The Bible tells us that whatever we give we will receive back tenfold, and this works in relationships as well. Do you ever wonder why some people have so many friends and they always seem to be such social butterflies? To find the answer, all you have to do is watch how they treat their friends and spouses.

Learn to say I am sorry. One of the biggest relationship killers is the inability to admit when you're at fault and apologize. Do you have the ability to forgive a wrongdoing and put it behind you, or do you carry a grudge and refuse to let go of the hurt and pain someone else has caused you? How we respond to difficult experiences in life directly affects our spiritual and physical well-being. Many lives are ruined by bitterness or a lack of forgiveness. People go through physical and emotional breakdowns, because they refuse to forgive other people. The longer we carry a grudge, the heavier it becomes and the more it costs us.

How important is it to love oneself? Is it possible to give

fully of yourself to others, your family and your friends, if you don't love yourself? How we feel about ourselves directly affects how we relate to others. Those who are comfortable with the way they look and feel have a confidence that shows when they interact with others. They seem self-confident, secure, and friendly, while those who are unhappy with themselves seem to show more insecurity, mistrust, resentment, or animosity when relating with people.

It may seem pretty straightforward, but if we're not happy with ourselves, how can we be happy with others? And it's not all about appearance. There are many people, famous and otherwise, who aren't conventionally beautiful or handsome, but who exude a certain 'charm' that affects those around them. This comes from within, and it is that which makes them beautiful or desirable.

What kinds of spiritual relationships do you have? Do you pray daily and go to church weekly? Or do you pray when you need or want something and go to church twice a year at Easter and Christmas? Do you pray at all? Do you believe in a God(s)? Do you believe in a higher power or force?

Be a great communicator

Do your family, friends, or co-workers say that you don't listen to them? Do your children say to you, "I told you last week that I had…" Effective listening is like an art; it takes practice. Next time you're in a conversation, really try to listen. Look the other person in the eyes and nod occasionally so they know they are being heard. If the conversation is one you might have heard before, if you listen intently you will probably hear something that you have not heard before.

In the practice of consulting and coaching, one of the main challenges I have seen in most corporations, is a "top-down" communication deficiency. Many companies are run by entrepreneurs. Most entrepreneurs are visionaries, and the challenge with visionaries is that they *see* it in their head, but many fail to put their "visions" on paper for others to see as well. In my experience as a consultant and coach, I have found in many companies run by entrepreneurs, that communication from the top down barely exists. For example, I was hired as a coach for an owner of a company with great entrepreneurial spirit, but Austin often wondered why his was the only car still at the office at 7:00 pm. I had a chance to talk to his employees, and after talking to all five of them, I found I'd been given five different answers to what they thought the company did, and its mission. So unless you have mastered the art of mind reading, put your thoughts and mission on paper for all to see and buy into.

Managing your states

Most of us have triggers that take us from one state of being to another. How we manage our states is what makes us different from one another. We have all heard of dressing for success, and for some of us, putting on a suit makes us feel powerful and elevates us into a different state. How we dress and how we stand, or more importantly, how we think, can instantly change our state. "State" management is also an art you can develop, with a little patience. When you feel unstoppable, how exactly do you feel? What do you look like? What thoughts go through your mind? What do you say to yourself? What is your breathing like? How do you move? What does your voice sound like? Many people cannot manage their states so they turn to drugs and alcohol for state management. For me, I look at problems as challenges, so rather than saying I have a big problem here, I say I have a big [challenge here.] My mind and body both go into a different state and say, "Let's take it on." I then spend more time on the solution, rather than the challenge itself. Find out what your state management triggers are and play with them. Learn to put your self into that powerful state just by some type of gesture or anchor.

Don't forget to have fun!

Ever feel that life is like being on a hamster wheel? Everywhere we look, people are chasing success. Success means different things to different people, but for the majority, it means acquiring possessions and money. Well, I say, *stop*! Look around! You may be there already! Enjoy where you are now! Have some FUN! Treat yourself and your family. You deserve it. The statistics say that the number of people who hate their job is staggering! I say, *quit* and do something you like, or better yet, something you're good at.

You know the old saying about the person on their death bed wishing that they had spent more time at the office? Yeah, right!

About Robert A. Arthurs

Born in Edmonton, Alberta in 1958, I developed my entrepreneurial skills early. At the age of 10, I was selling Regal Cards door to door. At 12 years I had a paper route with 120 houses on my list, and whether it was 40 degrees below or 100 degrees above, everyone got their paper for the next four years.

At 16 I worked at a gas station, pumping gas after high school. I continued to work at that station and commenced an apprenticeship as a mechanic. On the day I was to start the second year of school for my mechanic apprenticeship, I was involved in a serious motorcycle accident, which ended my career as a mechanic. In fact, it ended my career as anything for the next year.

At 21, after healing, I took a job driving a truck and making deliveries. At 23 I bought my own truck and went into oilfield delivery (hotshot). Then the economy in Alberta went sour, all the oil rigs left, and I closed up my business. At 24 I took a job in human resources, and for the next 10 years I would coordinate non-union workers (sometimes up to 300 workers) onto union job sites all over Alberta for oil refinery shutdowns. At 28 I started a 10-month entrepreneurial night course at N.A.I.T, where I wrote a business plan on starting a maid service. Once the course was completed, I started my own business, Sweeping Beauties Inc., part time in the YMCA incubator center. Eventually, with all the press we were getting and the way the business was growing, I was able to leave my human resources job to run Sweeping Beauties Inc. full-time. With the success of this company I decided to open up in North Vancouver. After two short years in Vancouver, I decided to close Edmonton and sell the BC operations to pursue what I saw as a need in the market for a T-shirt that said "Canada" tastefully, and was not made in China. The Company was to be True North Clothing Co. Inc. The "need" arose after the defeat of the Meech Lake & Charlottetown Accord, when most people thought the country was going to break up. So we came out with a shirt that said TRUE NORTH STRONG & FREE, with the flag on it. Sales exceeded my dreams, (we'd hit peoples' emotions about Canada). Today, True North has 450 retailers carrying our products worldwide, and we were voted No. 1 from 100 of the fastest growing businesses in Canada this century.

I have been nominated three times for the Ernst & Young Entrepreneur of the Year award: in 1994, 1997, and 1999. I was also nominated for Vancouver City's Business Ethics in Action award for my non-profit work. I have been invited to speak all over Canada and in the USA, sharing my stories and experiences. Today I am Certified Coach & Business Consultant/ Trainer. I have a company called Consultant-Coach.com. I work with business owners and upper management, Consulting/Coaching in their business lives, while Coaching in the personal lives to bring about balance and harmony in both worlds.

Some experiences I have had the pleasure of while learning about business include:

Several types of litigations; Trademark infringement; Trademark usage; buying another Trade Mark; Trade Mark Section 45; negotiations of all types; creditor arrangements; employee hiring & dismissal; business plan writing; finding an investor; bank financing; going to court for disputes in the capacity of the defendant and the plaintiff; involvement in audits of all types; ethical business practices; exporting to USA, Germany, and Japan; working with quota & TPL programs for NAFTA; and importing from Taiwan.

I have also participated in approximately two hundred trade shows in Canada, USA, and Japan, and I have been on two trade missions to Japan, and one to China.

3

The Vision and the Venture: Turning Dreams Into Reality

by Laura Terrebonne

"Goals are the result of bringing dreams, ideas, and ideals into tangible and examinable form."
PETER J. DANIELS

"The vision must be followed by the venture. It is not enough to stare up the steps - we must step up the stairs."
VANCE HAVNER

Leigh called me bright and early the first working day of the New Year. Her voice was filled with excitement and energy. I could tell that she was smiling both inside and out.

"I want to reach a few goals," she said. "A friend of mine said that you could help me do that. When can we get started?"

After a few minutes spent getting to know Leigh, I discovered that she really wanted this year to be different from years past. This epiphany had occurred a couple of days earlier, when she and a friend were discussing their respective resolutions for the upcoming year. Leigh suddenly realized that her resolutions had been the same year after year.

Many of my coaching clients tell me about their plans, their

27

dreams and goals, and their struggles to achieve them. The frustration is evident in their voices. In spite of all their good intentions, and even good efforts, somehow the desired results just don't seem to follow. This struggle is precisely what brings most clients in search of me.

We began the process of examining Leigh's goals. I asked her to write each one out on a sheet of paper. The simple act of writing them down "did something that made [them] seem more real", Leigh later told me. Her goals were fairly typical ones:

- Start my own business.
- Have more fun.
- Get into better physical shape.
- Get out of debt.

There was nothing about her goals that was unrealistic or unattainable, and yet there seemed to be a huge gap between where she was and where she wanted to be. Why had Leigh suffered the same disappointing results year after year? What was stopping her from achieving her dreams?

What's Holding You Back?

Think about all the resolutions you've made. How many of them have you kept? Why does it seem so easy to make resolutions or set goals, yet so difficult to follow through on them? We have every intention of keeping them. We may even manage to achieve a few, but we often find ourselves in the same predicament as Leigh – making the same promises to ourselves year after year. If this pattern continues unabated, we may begin to create a cycle in our lives of making promises, resolutions, or setting goals with either half-hearted, or no follow-through, and disappointing results. At best, it can simply become a ritual we observe with no real intention of taking action, or at worst, an exercise in futility leading to discouragement, self-doubt, and repeated failures.

Does this scenario sound a bit too familiar for comfort? Don't feel too badly; you're in good company. I'd be willing to bet that most everyone reading this has found himself or herself in a place like this more than once. The good news is that once you realize where you are, you can get to where you want to be. So, what's holding you back? Are you ready to take this incredible journey to learn how to both set and REACH your goals and dreams? Fantastic! Let's get started.

Dream Big

Every great (and small) invention or creation begins with a dream. In 1968, Don Wetzel was waiting in line at a Dallas, Texas bank dreaming of a way he could get his banking done quicker. One year later, he and two other men, Tom Barnes and George Chastain, developed the first working prototype of the Automatic Teller Machine (ATM). Clarence Crane had been dreaming of a candy that would withstand the summer heat of Cleveland, Ohio when he invented "Life Savers" candy in 1912. These men had a goal, and that goal began with a dream.

You are no different. From the time you were very young, you had dreams, desires, and wishes – some probably totally outrageous. Yet, that really didn't matter, did it? Think back and remember the times you spent "daydreaming" about becoming a world famous ballet dancer, or movie star, or whatever. You probably even made up games and role-plays to "live out" your fantasies. "Child's play!" the little voice in your head says. "I'm a realist now – no time for such idleness." Too bad. Somewhere in our growing up and getting smarter, we've lost the simple, child-like ability to dream big. Maybe this is one reason why as many as 83 percent of working people are thoroughly dissatisfied with their jobs or careers, according to some surveys. We tend to "drive" ourselves towards the things that we think we want, which can be very emotionally and physically costly. Goals alone tend to "drive" us forward. Dreams, however, can become the matrix on which we build our vision, which, in turn, will continually "draw" us forward.

The first step in setting goals is to dream – and dream big. Try this:

> Find a quiet place where you won't be disturbed for several minutes. Just sit quietly and let your mind run free. Dream really big. Think of everything you want. You might even think back to when you were younger and remember some of those "daydreams" that you squashed as you became more of a "realist". Don't worry about whether or not it's realistic or achievable – leave that for later. Forget the rules and boundaries. Right now, just have fun. It will be beneficial for you to write down your dreams as they come to you – perhaps in a journal. Write down everything that comes to your mind. Getting the dream from your mind and heart and onto paper is an important first step towards making your dream a reality. Write down exactly what you want. Be specific. If writing is not your "forte", try other ways of getting your dream out into the open – a photo collage, an audio or video tape of yourself relaying your dream, or whatever works best for you. The important thing is to express your dream.

As you do this exercise, you may hear that little "voice" in your head start to say something like, "You can't do THAT!" or, "This will be too hard to accomplish." As best as you can, still that voice for now. Put aside those beliefs that you "can't" or "shouldn't" or "don't deserve it". Just imagine that you've been given a "blank check" and nothing is out of your reach. This time is for being creative. The work will come in due time. Don't rush through this part – get as much down on paper as you want.

Leigh's big dream was financial independence. To her that meant having enough income to live on for two years. With that, she could "walk away" from any job she didn't find fulfilling if she chose to, without worry. She expressed her dream in a photo collage that she put up in her bathroom in front of the toilet! "That way," she told me later, "it's the first thing I see in the morning, and the last thing I see at night."

Now that Leigh had her "big" dream and had expressed it, we could get to work on the "nuts and bolts" of turning her dream into a goal, and the goal into reality.

Get real

Once you have your dream out in the open, you need to step back and take a look at it. Analyze it. This is the process of turning your dreams into a realistic, achievable goal. Start by asking yourself some probing questions. For example:

- *What does my dream mean to me?* Give your dream a little "meat". Define some of the tangibles of your dream. Do you really want to own your own business, or simply have more flexibility and independence in your current job?
- *What impact will this have on my life?* How will your life be different when you achieve your dream? How will you be different? In order to make this a reality you must believe in it. That means counting the cost and being willing to pay the price.
- *What are my values?* Values are who we are. They are the compass around which we orient our lives. When we honor our values, our lives are fulfilling. Our goals must then honor our values or we will find ourselves working for things that do not bring true satisfaction and joy to our lives.
- *Is this achievable?* Making a million dollars in six months is a nice dream – not entirely realistic - but nice. Making a million dollars in five years is more achievable. Don't set yourself up for failure before you start.
- *What are the barriers?* What are the potential obstacles that could impede your progress towards

your goal? What has stopped you from achieving it so far? Knowing what may get in your way helps you plan your route better.

Leigh and I looked at her dream of financial independence and worked through some of the questions above. She had already identified what her dream meant to her – having enough money saved to live on for two years, being able to walk away from any unfulfilling job, and freedom.

Having this kind of freedom would allow her to fulfill a real desire of hers – starting her own business. She had long wanted to be able to work in an environment that was consistent with her own values, but often found herself at odds with corporate "policies". Owning her own business would give her the freedom of being her own boss and creating the kind of environment in which she could thrive. This was her heart's desire. She knew what she needed to start and run a successful business, but had been financially tied to her current job. It seemed that no matter how hard she tried, she was unable to save enough money from each paycheck to get her any closer to her dream.

Can you see Leigh's dream beginning to take shape? By answering questions like these, you will notice that your dream is becoming more tangible; more defined. Now you are ready to begin the process of setting actual goals.

Get serious

Turning your dreams into goals is a very exciting part of this process. This is the beginning of crafting the plan that will move you closer to making your dream a reality. Don't rush through this part. This can be either a "stepping stone" or a "stumbling block" as you begin your journey. Here are some tips to setting well-crafted goals:

- *Make your goals "action" oriented and not "outcome" oriented.* You can't control the outcome, but you can control your actions. To say, "I will earn $2000.00 in sales commission this month" is not easily controlled. However, to say, "I will make 20 new contacts this week" is something you can more easily control.
- *Make your goals in the present tense.* State your goal as if you've already attained it. "I vacation in Europe for one month each year." If you think only of your goal in the future tense, your sub-conscious mind will keep it there. You want it to be here and now.
- *Make your goals your own.* Center your goals on your passions and not someone else's expectations of you. If you believe in what you do, you will create focus, motivation, and direction. A half-hearted effort is pointless and counter productive.
- *Make your goals realistic.* Consider the cost and what you're willing to pay. It would be very difficult to earn $150,000.00 a year if you're only willing to work two hours a day. Again, don't set yourself up for failure before you begin.
- *Make your goals balanced.* Having a focus is good. Being too focused can be detrimental. Remember, this is only a part of the whole of your life. Keep room in your life for other important people and things.
- *Write down your goals.* Keeping them only in your mind keeps them too vague (and easily forgotten). Keep them in a conspicuous place so they will stay in the forefront of your mind. Remember Leigh's photo collage?
- *Be specific.* Having a goal of "more time with my family" is vague and lends itself to non-specific action. "I spend one hour each evening reading to my children," gives you a focus and a tangible outcome to aim for.
- *Be positive.* State your goals in a positive sense. Instead of saying, "I will lose 30 pounds," say, "I am at my ideal weight of 120 pounds." We tend to respond better to the positive than to the negative.

You might also consider setting long, medium, and short-range goals. This is an excellent way to break down a big task or goal into smaller, more "do-able" pieces and avoid getting bogged down. Long-range goals should be broad and inspiring: "I am the top selling agent for the mid-western region this year." Medium-range goals break down the inspiration into measurable objectives: "Increase sales by 15% over last year." Short-range goals then break the medium-range goals into task steps: "I make five sales calls each day."

After working through this exercise, Leigh's goals looked like this:

> Long-range goal – I am financially independent. I own a business that reflects my values and passions. What I do each day brings me real joy and fulfillment.
> Medium-range goal – I have two years worth of my current income saved. ($106,000.00)
> Short-range goal – I put $1400.00 into my savings account each month.

Now Leigh had not only a dream, but also the foundation of a plan to get her from where she was to where she wanted to be. She had the vision to draw her forward and knew what it would take to get there. Next came the "action steps" she needed to take to achieve her short-range goal.

Get busy

Once you have clearly defined goals down on paper, the next step is to develop a plan to attain them. Everything you've done thus far has been the "what", "why", and "when" of goal setting. Now comes the "how". This is where things might seem to get a bit overwhelming. After all, you have decided to tackle this HUGE endeavor and will most likely be asking yourself at this point, "Now what?"

That first step can seem to be the biggest and most difficult one to make. It's all right to have this feeling. It's a perfectly normal one. Remember though what Emerson said about the journey of a thousand miles? Right. It begins with a single step. Ready? Take a deep breath and let's take that step

You will need to identify the resources you have available to you that will help you attain your goal. These may include time, energy, money, commitment, friends, or a network. Ask yourself these questions: What resources do you need? How can these resources be of benefit to you? How can you maximize these resources? For example, let's say that your goal is to write a book that you will submit to be published. How much time each day do you have to spend writing? Do you know anyone else that writes professionally? Are they willing to give you technical advice? What type of computer software do you have to help with the project? What publishers will you submit your work to? You will also need to identify resources that you need but do not yet have. What will you do to obtain these?

After you've identified the resources you have (or need), you will need to decide on a time frame and some specific actions you will take to reach your goal. These should be concrete. Going back for a moment to our earlier example of writing a book, you might set a time frame of six months to complete the project. You decide that you can spend two hours writing each evening. You may even have a definite number of words or chapters that you set as your target each week. You will also spend one evening each week at the library or on the Internet researching publishing companies. The point is to be very specific about what you will do and when it will be completed. Make your steps small enough to attain but also big enough to "stretch" you a bit. Have regular "checkpoints" built in to your plan to measure your progress and make adjustments. It's also important to reward yourself for each accomplishment. This is hard work and you deserve a pat on the back. Have fun along the way! Remember that you do not have to do this alone. Yes, you hold the vision and the passion for getting this done, but you will need the support of others. Having a support system like friends, family, or a personal coach is very important. They can be there for moral support, guidance, or that "kick in the pants" we all need from time to time in order to keep us moving forward.

Leigh had set a time frame of six years to accumulate two year's worth of salary and knew that she needed to set aside $1400.00 each month in her savings account to attain that goal. In our coaching sessions, I began asking her questions like, "What can you do to save that amount each month?" We broke her goal down even a bit more. "How much do you need to save each week?" "Each day?" "What do you need to do in order to save that amount?"

Through this type of question and answer format, we identified several things Leigh could easily do in order to save the money she needed each month. In the process, Leigh learned a lot about herself and what truly made her happy. She found that she had more energy and creativity as she explored new ways of living life. At first, it was difficult and she sometimes failed to meet her small goals. However, she kept the "big dream" in front of her and let it continue to draw her forward. With every success, she rewarded herself and we celebrated each as a victory.

As you proceed through this process, you will need to have "checkpoints" built in along the way. These will give you the opportunity to look at where you are in the process as well as how far you've come on the journey. You may need to make adjustments to your goals or to your plan. That's okay. Keep your "big dream" up in front of you, and it will be easy to reset your "compass" as you orient your life towards achieving your dream. It will be very beneficial for you to keep a record of your journey, such as a journal, so that you can track your progress. Who knows? That could even turn into your book someday.

The outcome

Leigh is well on her way to achieving her life's dream of financial independence and of owning her own business. The job she once hated now has meaning. She realizes that it is part of the means to achieving her financial freedom. Her attitude towards things and people is changing dramatically. Does she meet her goals each and every month? No. What she does do, however, is to continue to make substantial forward progress in spite of the occasional setbacks she may encounter. She has learned how to self-correct her steps when she comes up against life's "detours". What once absolutely threw her for a loop, she now welcomes as another opportunity to explore and learn about herself and discover new ways to take those steps that bring her ever closer to her dreams. She now has a focus and a passion for her life and starts every day with new excitement.

During one of our recent coaching sessions, Leigh said to me, "You know, I probably could have done all this without your help." I was silent – a little taken aback. Then she continued, "But I wouldn't have." It was the nicest compliment she could have paid me. The real credit, however, goes to Leigh. She did the hard part. This year has been different for her than past years – all because she was willing to dream big, set her goals, then take that first step.

What about you? I'll bet you have big dreams too. Are you ready to set your course and start that incredible journey towards making that dream a reality? You can do it, you know. You really can. What are you waiting for? C'mon, stop just staring up those stairs, and take that first step.

About Laura Terrebonne

Certified Comprehensive Coach, Laura Terrebonne, is a vibrant, energetic, and successful business and personal coach, financial analyst, and communication specialist. As founder of Success Alliance, a coaching and financial planning business, she coaches clients through change management, career transition, business growth and organizational and team development. In addition to Fortune 500 companies, regional and local businesses, executives, and professionals in many fields, Laura also coaches small business owners and families helping them take control of their financial future.

Laura is also Director of Operations for Comprehensive Coaching U, where she trains others in the art of coaching and works side by side with Terri Levine, founder of Comprehensive Coaching and author of *Work Yourself Happy.*

Laura is an outstanding member of the coaching community and has authored numerous articles which have appeared in publications such as *The Small Business Journal, Women Entrepreneurs Online Network, Bird Business Monthly, Better Business Focus, and Money Monthly.*

She and her husband, David, along with their beloved dog Otis, make their home in Tennessee and can be reached at:

(931) 484-6290

Laura@SuccessAllianceCoaches

http://www.SuccessAllianceCoaches.com

4

Reaching for New Heights

by Chris Wyle

"Your vision has created your desire. Your desire has created your momentum, and your momentum will determine your success."
CHRIS WYLE

Success does not happen by accident. Success is planned. Ask any one of the world's most successful people - Bill Gates, Tiger Woods, Bill and Hilary Clinton. They all had a plan worked out; meticulously followed to the line. Have you got a plan already worked out? Have you got a plan for your success? How do you intend to create an abundance of those good things in your life? Without a plan, where are you going? It is extremely difficult to get somewhere if you have no idea of how to get there. It is like saying, "Come to my house", without me giving you any idea of where I live, apart from maybe the name of the town, and without having a map. "Just set out in your car and drive to my house." You would have no chance of getting there, because you don't know how to get to where you are going. That is what it is like with goals, dreams, aspirations, or desires. You must have a plan mapped out, just like you would have your route map worked out, and follow it every turn; every left and every right; follow it to the line. Eventually, you will get to my house. Eventually, you will get to where you want to be, in a place where you will get an abundance of good things in your life.

There are two ways to create unlimited success in your life. The first is trial and error, and the second is to mimic successful people. The most effective method, by far, is to mimic the most successful people. Take this analogy and consider success to be the baking of a perfect cake. If I had baked the most perfect cake in the world and you wanted to emulate my achievements, would you pick up any old recipe book and start working through it to bake that cake? If you did, you probably wouldn't get the same result as me, because the only way you can get the same result, that being the most perfect cake in the world, is to copy exactly what I did. Copy the exact ingredients, the exact heat of the oven, the same length of cooking time, and the same length of time needed to let the cake cool down. Follow what I have done exactly to the line; mimic it *exactly*. That is the only way to copy true success. So if you find people in your field of expertise, or the field in which you want to work, locate those who are already successful in that field and copy what they do. Trial and error may get you there in time, but it will take a lot longer than if you were to use proven techniques and strategies for success. So how passionately do you want it? How quickly do you want it? Do you want it now? Do you want it today? If you do, you have to copy what's been done before.

Let's go back to my earlier quote: "Your vision has created your desire." Let's take a look at vision. We have all heard of the world's most famous theme park- Disneyland. Walt Disney, the creator of Disneyland, had a vision, and that vision is what millions of people see today in Disneyland, Disney World, and the Epcot Center. On the opening day of the Epcot Center, a reporter said to Walt Disney's cousin, (because unfortunately, Walt Disney had passed away), "I guess this is a bittersweet day for you." Walt's cousin said, "Why do you say that?" The reporter replied, "Walt Disney is not here to see this." His cousin turned back to the reporter and said, "Walt saw it, and that's why you're seeing it today." Walt Disney was so vivid in his imagination and so descriptive in his vision that we are able to see exactly what he saw years before. He set himself goals. He was very descriptive of his goals; very detailed with his goals.

Goals are extremely powerful and are an essential part of creating unlimited success in our lives. Do you have goals? Or more to the point, do you have written goals? A goal is not a goal if it is not written down; it is just a dream, but when it is written down it becomes a plan; a plan of action, which then becomes an action plan for your success.

How powerful can goals be? The answer to that is *extremely* powerful. There was a case study in 1953, when the graduating class of Yale University were all interviewed. As part of this research, the class of 1953 were asked how many of them had written goals; clearly written goals for their future. It was found that only 3% of the class had. Twenty years later, the surviving members of the class of 1953 were interviewed again, and it was found that the 3% of the class who had clearly written goals for their future were worth more financially than the other 97% put together. That is the power of goals; the power of clearly written goals. Financial success was used as a measure in this case, as it is the easiest benchmark to measure.

I have talked about following and copying success; copying what's been done before. Many successful people have followed this route to achieve their dreams, and detailed below, this route is set out for you. There are 10 steps to guaranteed success, and if you follow these steps to the line, you will create an abundance of everything you want in your life.

Step 1 - Vision
Like Walt Disney, see what you want and detail it in your mind; see it, feel it, taste it, and enjoy it. Try to make the feelings as real as possible. This is building up the desire; it is almost

building up a *need* for those things in your life. It is also about belief. Believe in yourself unquestionably and unequivocally, and you will succeed. You will attain the targets you have set yourself and begin to live the life you deserve.

Consider this true story about belief and self-belief. We have all heard of the famous movie star Sylvester Stallone. Well, at one time, Sylvester Stallone wasn't quite as successful as he is today. In fact, he was failing as an actor and failing in life miserably. He lived in a one bedroom apartment with his best friend in the world, his dog Butkiss. He was broke, he had little food, and he could not pay for heating. However, he had a dream, a passion, and that was to become a movie star. Sylvester Stallone went to audition after audition to get a role in a movie. Turned down time after time, people kept saying to him, "Your nose is bent, your lip sticks up, and you can't act." He received rejection, after rejection, after rejection.

Sylvester Stallone went to numerous auditions through this period of hardship, and nobody would take him on. But he would not give up on his vision; his dream of becoming a movie star. So he persevered, going to audition after audition, and even though he had little food and no heating, he still kept trying. In fact, it got to the point that he was so destitute that he had to sell his dog; he had to sell Butkiss, and he sold him outside an off-license for $15 just so he could buy some food - he was that desperate to eat. Sylvester Stallone kept trying, and he kept failing; he kept being rejected; he kept being turned down. So what did he do? He did not give up; he changed his approach. Instead of quitting, he thought to himself, "Right then, these auditions aren't working. What other way can I get to be an actor? What other way can I get to be a movie star? I know, I'll write a film." So Sylvester Stallone wrote a film. You might have heard of it: "Rocky". It's about an American boxer. When he took this film, "Rocky", to producers, directors, and studios to see if they wanted to make it, again he was rejected, and he was rejected for two reasons this time: firstly, because they didn't believe in the "Rocky" story, and secondly, because they didn't want Sylvester Stallone to act in the film (because Sylvester's first condition was that he play Rocky.)

One studio took Sylvester up on the idea and offered him $125,000 NOT to play Rocky. Bear in mind that $125,000 was a lot of money, particularly as Sylvester had recently sold his best friend so that he could eat. It is a lot of money for someone who lives in a one bedroom apartment with no heating, but he turned down this $125,000 *not* to play Rocky because he was so adamant that he *would* play Rocky. Negotiations continued, and the film company offered him $250,000 *not* to star in his own film, but still he rejected the offer. In the end, they settled on an agreement for $30,000, with Sylvester Stallone playing Rocky and receiving a percentage of the takings. With this $30,000, Sylvester went back to the off-license where he had sold his dog, and he waited night after night for the man who had purchased Butkiss to come back, and eventually he did. Sylvester said to this man, "I was desperate, I was hungry, I was cold, and I had to sell my dog to get some money, but now I have some money and would like to buy my dog back." He offered the man his $15 back, but the man refused. He offered him $30, and the man still refused. So then he offered him $100, but again, the man refused. Finally, Sylvester Stallone bought Butkiss back for the sum of $15,000 and a walk-on part in "Rocky" for the man to whom he had sold the dog. Today, Sylvester Stallone is one of the most successful movie stars in history. "Rocky" made him a multimillionaire, and all of this because he had a dream, he had a plan, he persevered, and he would not quit.

Can you persevere like Sylvester Stallone? Have you got a vision like Walt Disney?

Step 2 – Set your own goals

Do what you want; not what you believe others expect of you. You are in control of your destiny; do not let other people try to control it for you. If you are passionate about something, if you believe beyond a shadow of a doubt that you can achieve something, do not let other people interfere with your goals.

Set your own goals. After all, it is your life, and if you should allow others to dictate to you, there is a strong possibility that you will regret their domination later in your life.

Step 3 – Set deadlines for the achievement of your goals

It's important to have an end date. It's important to have an end date because it sharpens your focus. You need to set a final deadline for completion of your major goals and also short-term deadlines along the way, milestone deadlines if you like, so that you know you are progressing to your ultimate destiny.

Step 4 – Discuss your goals with a supportive partner

I recommend that your Supportive Partner be a Life Coach; someone who will prompt you; someone who will provide that spur when the going gets tough; someone who you will be accountable to for your actions; someone who will be as committed to your success as you are. It's very hard to do it on your own; it's a tough world out there. Get some help. A Life Coach is the perfect partner; they will assess your inner goals to ensure that you are striving for a goal that you truly desire. Your Life Coach will ensure that you remain on course with a focused direction, listen enthusiastically to the challenges you face, and celebrate with you when you overcome these challenges.

Step 5 – Do something immediately towards the attainment of your target

If your target is to own a Mercedes - order a brochure. If your target is to buy a new house – find out how much houses are selling for. Find out mortgage rates. Find out if you can get a mortgage. If your target is to be more confident, or to be able to stand up and give a presentation in front of 30 people – get a Life Coach, but get one today. Do something immediately towards the achievement of that goal, and if for some reason you cannot do it immediately, you must do something within the next 12 – 24 hours. Success will not come and find you,

you have got to get up, do something new, and persevere. "If you do what you have always done, you will get what you have always got."

Step 6 – Be prepared to give up things that are barriers to your goal

For instance, if your goal is to be fit and healthy and you are a smoker, then you need to quit smoking. If your goal is to lose weight, but all you ever eat is take-away food, you need to change your diet. So be prepared to give up anything that is a barrier towards your goal. It may seem difficult and more like some sort of punishment to begin with, but if you continually focus on the reasons why you are doing it, and the outcome of your efforts, you will discover that it may have been short-term pain for long-term satisfaction and fulfilment.

Step 7 – Be prepared to change your approach if what you are doing is not working

Let's reflect back to the Sylvester Stallone story. Despite audition, after audition, after audition, he did not get a job as an actor. He thought, "This isn't working, so what else can I do?" So he wrote his own story, and eventually he succeeded. Don't be afraid to change tactics if you need to.

Step 8 – Persist

Even when the going gets tough and the achievement of the goal appears further away than ever, keep going; dig your heels in; this is when a Life Coach comes into their own. This is a time when the support that a Coach provides for you is invaluable. Think back again to the Sylvester Stallone story. If he had quit after the tenth audition, after the fiftieth audition, or even after the one hundredth audition, would he be where he is today?

Let's take a look at the story of Thomas Edison, the man who invented the electric light bulb. After five thousand attempts to create the electric light bulb, someone said to him, "Look Edison, you are crazy. You have failed five thousand

45

times; why don't you just quit?" Edison turned to his friend and said, "I haven't failed five thousand times. I have found out five thousand ways not to invent the electric light bulb." And he went on to invent the electric light bulb at the five thousand and first attempt. How many of us would persist to the degree that Thomas Edison did?

Step 9 – Celebrate

Celebrate every success along the way, every milestone along the way, and have a major party when you achieve your goal. It's important to have something to look forward to. It is important to be grateful, and be thankful, for everything you achieve. Learn to develop the attitude of gratitude.

Step 10 – Set more goals

Don't become stagnant. Do not become boring and ordinary. Constantly strive to achieve more, because if you stay with what you have today, tomorrow it will be worth less. Have something to aim for, a purpose in life, new challenges to overcome, and new triumphs to be celebrated.

Remember, the two most important things to the achievement of your goals are belief and persistence.

Let's consider belief for a moment. We have all heard of Roger Bannister, the first man to break the four minute mile. Well, across the Pacific Ocean in Australia, there was an athlete named John Landy who was reported as saying that no human could run a mile faster than four minutes, because if you do your heart will seize up and your bones will break. Can't be done; it's impossible! Roger Bannister did not believe this. Roger Bannister believed that the four-minute mile could be broken and he broke it. Within days of Roger Bannister doing this, John Landy also broke the four-minute mile, and within a year, over 50 more runners from around the world broke the four-minute barrier. The reason for this: their belief had changed when they saw somebody else had done it, and they now knew it could be done.

Let's take another example. Have you ever heard of the Aboriginal Truth Test? If an Aborigine is suspected of lying, then a group is brought before the Chief and a hot poker is produced. The hot poker is placed on the tongue of each member of the group; the liar is the only person who gets his tongue burnt. That is because these Aborigines are bought up with the strong belief that if they lie, their tongue will be burnt, and if they are not lying, it will not. Commonsense tells us that if we have a hot poker on our tongue it will burn us, and for many of us it would, but because the Aborigines' belief is so strong, the poker will not burn them, and they will not suffer any discomfort if they are telling the truth.

Let's also take a look at persistence or momentum: continually striving, continually trying to achieve, changing your approach, changing your outlook, trying something new, and attempting something time and time again. Do you try something five times, or do you try ten times before you give up? You never know how close you are to success.

Think back to the story of Thomas Edison, who, after inventing the Electric Light Bulb, went on to patent over twelve hundred inventions. He did this with only three months of education in his whole life and no scientific training whatsoever. This clearly demonstrates that belief and commitment are more important ingredients for success than education and qualifications.

So let's review. The achievement of goals is down to your state of mind. Do you believe in your ability enough to make your wildest dreams come true? As Henry Ford said, "Whether you believe you can, or believe you can't, you are probably right." Have a plan and set goals. Failing to plan is like planning to fail. Be passionate, and be prepared to do the hard and necessary exercises to achieve your goals; not just the fun and easy parts. Get a Coach. This is a priority. A Coach will assist you, push you, provide that spur when the going gets tough, and celebrate with you when you achieve your goals. Believe in yourself unequivocally. You are better than you believe you are today; never let anybody ever tell you otherwise.

47

When we truly commit to something, a whole manner of things comes together. It's been said that human beings are like magnets, attracting the things in our lives we focus on most. If our conscious thoughts and sub-conscious thoughts are focused on achieving our goals and aspirations, then things that assist us to achieve these are drawn to us automatically. Don't ask me to explain it; it is just how Mother Nature works, so make sure that your mind is filled with positive thoughts and focused on the achievement of your objectives. Meditate daily and visualize the achievement of your objectives. Meditation is a powerful tool for creating unlimited success; it places your sub-conscious thoughts in tune with your conscious thoughts

Now you know what to do, but that's not enough. It has often been said that knowledge is power, and I could not disagree more with this statement. A correct way to phrase it is, "the implementation of knowledge is power." Millions of people around the world know what to do, but how many people do what they know? Go out there and put your plan into action.

Follow these steps to guaranteed success, and you will create an abundance of those things you so dearly desire. This is the success formula adopted by some of the most successful people in the world today. Why don't you join them? These goals will be achieved through having the vision, having the desire, sustaining the momentum, and celebrating every achievement along the way.

I wish you all success in the achievement of your goals. If there is any way I can help you, please contact REACH LIFE COACHING LTD.

About Chris Wyle and Reach Life Coaching

Reach Life Coaching is committed to providing the very highest level of Coaching, Training and support services for all of its clients.

Your decision to work with a Reach Life Coach could be one of the most positive and effective decisions you may ever make. Working with one of our professionally qualified Life Coaches can Turbo Boost your performance in many different areas of your life. Your Reach Life Coach can work with you on a wide variety of areas, helping you to overcome the challenges you face in your day-to-day life and celebrating with you the wins you have along the way. Below are listed just some of the many areas of your life that your Reach Life Coach can assist you with:

Confidence Building	Health and Fitness
Diet and Exercise	Career Development
Relationship Issues	Creativity
Self Esteem	Relaxation

At Reach Life Coaching Ltd., we believe that it is necessary for our Coaches to have a wide range of skills, and have practical experience in dealing with and enhancing performance and changing lifestyles, so that they may be as positively effective as possible. Therefore, all of our Coaches have achieved their accreditation from one, or in some cases, two of the top three Life Coach Training Providers in the world: The Life Coaching Academy, The International Coaching Federation, and Coach  University. As well as being qualified Coaches, we at Reach Life Coaching Ltd. look for something in our Coaches that really sets them apart from other Coaches. In order to provide additional benefits to our clients, Reach Life Coaching Ltd. have Coaches who are trained in the science of Neuro Linguistic Programming and also utilize the services of a Master Practitioner of Neuro Linguistic Programming. Our Coaches also have a wide range of experience in the training sector, having worked with some of the largest financial Institutions in the United Kingdom as Trainers, responsible for delivering courses on a wide range of topics including; sales, time management, change, values, and organization.

So if you are passionate about making a difference and committed to moving up to the next level, why not Reach out for something better in association with us.

For further details on our exciting range of Coaching, training, and support services, please contact us on 08707 414273, send an E-Mail to:

info@reachlifecoaching.com

or visit our Website at:

www.reachlifecoaching.com

"Your success is within Reach"

5

Finding Your Dharma[1] ...Your Passion... Your Purpose In Life

by Florence R. Rickards

A *ttempting to manifest that which we are not passionate about is like dressing up a corpse!*

If tomorrow you were diagnosed with terminal cancer and told you had only a few months to live, would the big house, the boat, the cottage at the lake, and the prestigious job title comfort you? Would you be wishing you had spent more time at the office? I think not. You might be wishing that you had dared to live your heart's longing, your dream…what you ached for…your passion…your purpose in life!

Doing what makes *your* heart sing, not what society says *should* make your heart sing, leads to a happy and fulfilling life. Why? Because when you are living from your heart and not from society's prescriptions, you open the floodgate to energy, commitment, inspiration, perseverance, joy, and fulfillment. Living your passion heightens your performance and enables you to achieve things you never dreamed possible.

Some time ago, a random sample of fifteen hundred graduating college seniors were surveyed to find out what they would base their career choice on. Eighty-three percent said that financial gain was the first thing they would base

[1] Dharma is a Sanskrit Word that means purpose in life.

50

their career choice on, and following their dream, their passion, would come second. Seven percent said that following their dream, their passion, would be first and financial gain second. In a follow-up study on actual net-worth twenty years later, they found that 101 of the 1500 students had become millionaires. But only one of those millionaires had come from the group who put financial gain first, while one hundred of them came from the group who put following their passion first.

The point is that a path with heart, and a purpose with passion driving it, is incredibly powerful. People who do great things have, above all else, a purpose that stirs their soul. So follow your dreams. Do what you are passionate about, and do it with all your heart and soul, and you will be happy, fulfilled, and successful.

Read on. Find out how to create a life, a real life, not a manic pursuit of the next promotion, the bigger pay cheque, or the bigger house. Find out how to discover what makes *your* heart sing. It's only too late if you don't start now.

Barriers to finding and living your passion

Why don't more of us live our passion? One reason is that many of us are so busy with our careers and the business of survival that we don't stop to think about what we are doing. We are living as human *doings* rather than human *beings*. Always busy, running here, running there, and not taking the time to be with ourselves. Think about it. When was the last time you spent an evening or an afternoon with yourself...just *being?*

Many individuals I coach tell me that they are not happy or fulfilled and that life has become dull. Still others comment, "There must be more to life than this". These individuals have accomplished much in their lives, and yet, they are still looking for something; something that fulfills, excites, motivates; something that makes them want to jump out of bed in the morning; something that gives their life meaning and purpose. But when I ask them what their passion is, or what their dreams are, they say they don't know. Not knowing what your purpose in life is, or what you are passionate about, can be a real barrier to living a life that makes your heart sing.

A number of individuals I have coached tell me they're too old or it's too late for them to find their passion. I've worked with people as young as 17 and as old as 64, and I have had people as young as 30 make the comment that "it's too late", or "I'm too old". This indicates that it is a matter of perspective and perception. The following story illustrates this. Three stonecutters were working in a quarry near a half-completed church. A traveller approached the three men and asked the first one what he was doing. The man complained bitterly, "I hate this work. My hands hurt, the stone flies in my face, and the hours are long and hard. For years I've been trapped in this hellish job." The traveller questioned the second man and he replied, "I work hard to support myself and my family. It's true that the hours are long, but it could be worse. I have no complaints." The third man was so intent upon his work that at first he did not even hear the traveller's question. The traveller persisted, and finally, the third stonecutter looked up and answered. His face was luminous. In a clear, gentle voice he replied, "I am building a cathedral." This story also shows that you can change the way you look at your situation, including your age, and the notion that it is too late. Thousands of individuals over the age of fifty find their passion in a new dream or a forgotten one. Our passions are intensely personal and change over time. What was important at age twenty-five may not be at age thirty-five; the empire building passion of thirty-five may give way to a search for something that will allow you to make a difference in the world at age forty-five or fifty. It is only too late if you don't start now. So start now!

Another barrier to pursuing one's passion is, "I can't". I recall a time in my life when there was a job I wanted, but it involved public speaking. I *knew* that I could not get up in front of a group and speak. As long as I *believed* that I could not do it,

I couldn't do it. Henry Ford once said, "Whether you *think* you *can*, or *think* you *can't,* you are right", and I was. It was only when I changed my mind, changed my *belief,* and started *believing* that I could get up in front of a group and speak, that I was actually able to do it. What I discovered is that to fulfill your dreams and live your passion, you must *believe* that you can.

Another roadblock to pursuing our passion is the anxiety we feel when we are in the field of uncertainty. Having a job with a regular pay cheque provides the illusion of certainty and security, but this means that you have closed the door to other options, opportunities, and ideas. If, on the other hand, you decide to quit your job and start your own business, you would be choosing to live in the field of uncertainty and you would open the door to other options and opportunities. However, being in this field is extremely uncomfortable, if not downright scary, for most people. Living a life of purpose and passion means learning to live in the field of uncertainty. One way of doing this is to change your view of the field. Start looking at the field of uncertainty as the *field of all possibilities.* When you are in the field of all possibilities, you become excited about the other opportunities. Your mind is open and creative and you put the law of attraction to work for you. When you do this, you are in a position of self-power and this draws people and things that you want to you. It magnetizes people, situations, and circumstances to support your goals and desires.

Probably the most significant and pervasive barrier to living your passion is your gremlins, the critics narrating in your head. Like most people, I have numerous gremlins running around in my mind. Whenever I try something new, or get excited, charged, motivated, and enthusiastic about some new idea, they come out in full force telling me all the reasons I *should not* go ahead with this great idea. They say things like, "you'll fail, you'll make a fool of yourself, everyone will laugh at you, they'll think you're stupid", and on and on they go. For years, my gremlins had free reign in my mind because I was not aware of them.

You can identify your gremlins by the words they use when they speak to you. For example, they use words like: should, have to, and ought to. Gremlins squelch your essence and your enjoyment. They criticize and condemn. They make you spend your time thinking about the past and worrying about the future. And as long as you are living in the past or the future, you are not living in the present. You are not *being* a human being. This is what your gremlins want. They are intent on making you feel lousy. They lead you into periods of anxiety, worry, fear, sadness, anger, depression, and emptiness. They perpetuate myths about you, other people, places, and things. For example, they will tell you that your true self is unlovable, that fast is good and slow is bad, getting angry is bad, you are not entitled to an opinion, asking for what you want is selfish, and so on.

One of the toughest gremlins to address is the victim gremlin. This narrating critic says things like: "this always happens to me; it's not my fault; if only my boss, my husband, my daughter would do such and such; or if only I had an education; more money...", and on and on it goes. This gremlin allows you to blame and justify rather than take responsibility for your life and your choices. This gremlin makes you helpless, hopeless, and powerless, not because of some circumstance, institution, or person, but because you end up giving your power away. As long as you listen to this gremlin you will stay stuck and not live your passion. To break free and live your passion...your purpose in life, you must first become aware of the role this gremlin is playing. Then you must take responsibility for your life and your decisions. Only then can you break free and choose to live your passion.

One way of taming your gremlins is by simply becoming aware of them. Notice them. Don't try to analyze or understand them. Simply notice them. This may sound simple, but just noticing, just becoming aware, is very powerful. When you do this, notice *how* you are, not *why* you are how you are. The reason this is so powerful is that you change not by trying to be something other than who you are, but by being fully aware of *how* you are.

Others know what their purpose in life is and are frozen in their tracks. Frozen with fear. Fear can cause us to feel pain, paralysis, and depression. Everyone experiences fear: fear of public speaking, of success, failure, asserting ourselves, intimacy, being alone, changing careers, ending a relationship, beginning a relationship, losing a loved one, leaving a job, or starting a business.

One way of conquering your fear is to acknowledge it for what it is. But what is fear? Fear is simply one of the ways that human beings *interpret* events. As the following story illustrates, fear can be a distorting lens. One afternoon, my neighbour was walking her German Shepherd, Sasha, down the street on a leash. Sasha has no interest in cats and usually leaves them alone. Crouching against a nearby building was a cat, keenly observing their approach. As they walked by the building, Sasha noticed the cat, but kept on walking. The cat, however, began arching his back, hissing and spitting. Suddenly, the cat launched himself at Sasha, all claws and teeth. In the brief, but violent, scuffle that ensued, Sasha was badly scratched, and the cat had his leg and ear bitten before my neighbour could separate them. The cat's fear was not generated by this situation, but by the cat. The cat could have stayed where he was and calmly observed my neighbour and her dog, Sasha, walk by. However, the cat was not capable of choosing his response. You are. Remember, courage is not the absence of fear, but going ahead in spite of your fear. When you realize that you are capable of choosing your response, you can overcome your fear. When you liberate yourself from your fears, the possibilities for building, shaping, and changing your life are endless.

Tools/Methods for finding your purpose in life... your passion

One way to find your purpose in life is to examine your values. When you are honouring your values, you are happy and fulfilled. You feel good. Hence, living a life according to what is important to you – your values, will lead you to your destiny. Unfortunately, many people do not know what their values are. The problem is that many of your values are there because they were important to someone else, your parents, teachers, clergy, friends, employers, and so on. When you were growing up, your parents supported and applauded you if you did things that agreed with their values and punished you verbally, physically, or emotionally if you did things that went against their values. The same was true of your teachers.

If you aren't sure what your values are, you can begin clarifying them now. The following is a partial list of values. Number them from one to ten in order of importance to *you*. If you want to live a life of passion and purpose, decide what you value most and then commit to living those values every day.

- Family
- Success
- Freedom
- Adventure
- Recognition
- Integrity
- Creativity
- Authenticity
- Personal power
- Security

Your decisions are guided by your values, and as such, direct your life. Therefore, when you know what your values are, life's choices and decisions become a lot easier. For example, when faced with a decision, you can ask yourself the following question: "Will this decision move me closer to honouring my values, or farther away?"

There are a number of ways to identify your values. One method is to think of a peak experience, a time when you felt happy, fulfilled, proud, energized, accomplished, and so on.

Then search the experience for the values that were being honoured. A second technique for identifying your values, is to go to the opposite extreme and think of experiences when you were angry, upset, or frustrated. This will identify values that were being violated or suppressed. Often we don't recognize values until something gets in the way of our honouring them.

A second way of finding your purpose in life is to use the no-fail/no-money fantasy exercise. For this technique, you simply write out your answer to the following question, being very specific and using as much detail as possible. If money was no object and you knew you could not fail, what would you do with your life? By examining your no-fail fantasy you will be able to identify some of your values and incorporate them into your life.

A third way of finding your purpose in life is to decide what you want your epitaph to say about you. For example, I want mine to say, "A trail blazer, she made a difference". How do you want to be remembered?

A fourth way of determining your life's purpose is to design a mission statement for yourself. Once you have done this, your mission statement will act like a huge neon sign, directing your life. To begin, start with an impact statement. What kind of impact do you want to have? For example, "I want people to be happy", or "I want to help people". Next, find a metaphor that captures the *essence* of your purpose. For example, "I am a lighthouse, or I am a trailblazer". Creating your mission statement takes time, so be patient with yourself. But get started. Remember, it's only too late if you don't start now.

Lastly, how do you find your passion? One sure fire way of finding out what you are passionate about is to identify the things that make your heart sing. When you are doing what you are passionate about, you:

- lose all track of time
- become energized and motivated
- are in the moment, not the past or the future
- feel fully alive, complete

- break down the barriers and overcome the fears that would otherwise stop you

Combining passion and purpose

If you are confused about passion and purpose, join the club. In talking to people about the link between passion and purpose, it was difficult to separate the two. The relationship between passion and purpose seems equal to the chicken or the egg question - which one comes first? Another question that arises is, are they always linked? I don't believe that they are. We have many passions in life, but they are not all linked to our purpose.

One thing is certain though, and that is that passion and purpose together create an incredibly powerful force! While watching a rerun of Martin Luther King's Speech "I have a dream", I was struck by the enormous amount of passion and conviction in his speech. It is no wonder that he moved a nation. On August 28, 1963, on the steps of the Lincoln Memorial in Washington, D.C., before a crowd of 250,000 people, Martin Luther King, Jr. proclaimed his dream to the world. Because this address was so powerful, it is still used today, almost thirty years later, in leadership programs throughout the world as an example of how leaders enlist others. This is a testimonial of the power of combining what you are passionate about with your purpose in life.

Tools/Methods for living your passion

Once you have identified your passion and your purpose, the next step is staying on track and living your passion...your purpose. In this busy, hectic society of ours, it is easy to get side tracked, off balance. Think about it. Most of us are living life in the fast lane. It is difficult to find time for family, friends, health, career, finances, your spouse, personal growth, spirituality, fun, and recreation. One way of recognizing that you are off balance is when your narrator, your gremlin, starts saying things like, "I can't, I have to, and I need to". When you are off balance, choice is gone and you are allowing yourself to be dictated to by circumstance. When balance is gone, the opportunity for fulfillment is gone.

Getting a personal coach is useful in maintaining balance. Anthony Robbins, Lee Iacocca, Dale Carnegie, Rick Hansen, Oprah Winfrey, and Ghandi all had a coach to mentor and guide them, to help them find their true potential, and to maintain balance in their lives. Behind every successful person there is someone who believes in them and challenges them to be all they can be! A coach will help you articulate your values, dreams, and purpose. They will also help you to realize when you are going against your values and assist you in maintaining your focus and life balance. Also, like athletes, we can all benefit from a cheering section in our lives. By cheering section, I mean people who nurture and support you, your passion, and your purpose. People who will cheer you on when the going gets tough. These could be friends, family, co-workers, your church, or a group you belong to. You will know which people in your life are your cheerleaders - your balcony people, because they will not condemn or criticize and they will root you on when you feel like throwing in the towel.

One final thought on living your passion and life's purpose is this - *We are not human beings having a spiritual experience; we are spiritual beings having a human experience.* Getting in touch with your spirit self is critical to finding and living your life purpose. People find their spirit self in different ways. It doesn't have to be through organized religion, or going to church; it's what works for you; it's what fills your heart. It could be a walk on the beach, a hike in the woods, prayer, a walk in a garden filled with beautiful flowers, listening to your favourite music, or meditation. Spend time with your spirit self, your true nature, every day, and as you do, your life's purpose will become clearer and stronger. You will spontaneously receive creative thoughts. You will be unafraid, calm, and peaceful. You will know what your life purpose is, what your unique gift to the world is, and you will be able to offer it freely. When you do, you will be validated and fulfilled, because the giving of your gift reaffirms the meaning of life. Listen to your heart, pay whatever it costs, and don't look back.

My parting wish for you is that you find your dharma...your passion...your purpose in life, and like Martin Luther King Jr., live your dream!

*God, give me the dream
that you planned for my life.*

About Florence R. Rickards

Florence Rickards is a dynamic, energetic, speaker, facilitator, and coach. She has over twenty years of experience assisting individuals & organizations in achieving their maximum potential, finding their passion, and realizing their dreams. She is currently President of *ACHIEVE* Consulting Inc., an organization that provides services in Training and Development, Human Resources, and Organizational Development. Her previous experience includes being the Creator/ Owner/Operator of a Private Training Institute, a Human Resources Generalist,
Personnel Manager, Director of Employee Support and Development, and Director of Business Development. She has worked in both the public and private sector.

Florence has a Masters Degree in Business Administration (Simon Fraser University), is a Certified Human Resources Professional, a Certified Vocational Rehabilitation Counsellor, and a Registered Social Worker. She is also a professional coach having received her training from the highly recognized Coaches Training Institute. In addition, Florence was the first faculty hired by the first Canadian campus of the University of Phoenix and teaches in both the Bachelor and Master of Business Programs. She received the teaching excellence award in 1999. Florence is also a sought after guest speaker and has presented at a number of local and International Conferences.

Florence is the President of the Canadian Mental Health Association—Simon Fraser Branch, a Director of NETWERCC (Networking, Education and Training for Workers in Employment, Rehabilitation and Career Counselling) since 1997 and an editor for the British Columbia Human Resource Management Association's PeopleTalk Magazine since 1997. She was recently awarded her own *Small Business Solutions* column for PeopleTalk. She is also the past Vice President of the Labor Market and Career Information Association of British Columbia.

Florence's passion is facilitating, guiding, motivating, inspiring, and energizing people and organizations on their journey to success and fulfillment. Florence has synthesized the best from psychology, human development, business, communications, mentoring, counseling, spirituality, and coaching to help individuals and organizations find and live their passion.

Florence can be reached at:

achieve@intergate.bc.ca

www.achieve-consulting.com

6

On the Leadership Ladder

by Diane Allen

"There is a special wisdom to collaboration, to success, to achievement, to delight. This wisdom can be found in one's inner spirit and through understanding the spirit of others."

DIANE ALLEN

The intense ego of the competitive spirit, the compassionate team builder, the courageous hero, the creative thinker, the structured planner. These traits are necessary ingredients for leaders at all levels. However, harnessing these traits and giving them meaning within the context of success can be more difficult than one would imagine.

Let us take a look at the case study of Chris, a new CEO of a national services firm. Through some insightful advice, courage, and use of a thinking styles/brain dominance profile, he was able to steer a wandering ship onto a course of success.

As a young executive, this brash MBA devoured every step of the career ladder. Starting out as a marketing manager, he was able to garnish the creative spirit in his organization and lead his division to a new high. Hand in hand, he worked with the product development group to position their Customer Relationship Management product before any other company gained market share. The impetus to develop a meaningful customer relationship management program was developed through his accurate understanding of business-to-business marketing and consumer behavior. He studied the marketplace and the technology, and led the service introduction in some high-powered industries. This paved the way for success. As one success led to another, Chris felt as though he had it all... power, influence, leadership, and a lucrative compensation package.

There was no doubt in anyone's mind that Chris could have it all. In just seven short years, he had become a senior vice president with a major division reporting to him. He had managed his way through Wall Street, understood the need for stellar returns to stockholders, and balanced that need with sound management practices. Why wouldn't he be chosen for Division CEO of a competitive company, even if he did seem a little young for the task?

Shortly after Chris took over, we found a different set of circumstances. The new company had declining market share, dwindling profits, high employee turnover, and the need to continue to invest. The former CEO was ousted because his values were stability and maintenance, over risk. That was okay for a while, but now times were different. The marketplace was slipping away. Something had to change. Chris had the magic touch and he understood the staid nature of the corporate culture. He inherited a management team of seemingly loyal followers. Collectively, the team had over 50 years of company experience. They would be his eyes and ears to manage through tough times. In fact, each of his team members confided to him how frustrated they had been getting with the former CEO for not reacting to the needed changes more quickly.

After two weeks, Chris assembled the management team for a daylong retreat. His agenda was to do a situation analysis of the company, including the external environment, new product development, employee satisfaction, and financial strategy. He expected to leave this retreat with a happy group who embraced some new strategic thinking and solid action plans. Instead, he left the meeting feeling a little out of control, confused, and unsure of how to proceed. What worked in other environments did not seem to be embraced here. He had a group of risk averse, structured executives who failed to see the need for his level of change management. He sensed they were reluctant to admit fear. Their silence was deafening. All of a sudden, his strong leadership characteristics that worked in other situations felt worn and ineffective.

Like all good leaders, Chris was wise enough to know when he could not or should not do something on his own. He called on a long time trusted coach who was always able to tell him what he *needed to hear - not what he wanted to hear*. Chris argued with himself about feeling insecure by needing his coach. On the other hand, he understood that the wisdom of good leadership is surrounding oneself with great resources.

As Chris discussed the events of the retreat with his coach, several things came to mind:

1) These executives worked together for a long time with a CEO who was very different from Chris.
2) They were a settled-in group unto themselves. Regardless of their expressed frustrations, they all remained loyal and chose not to change, even when those stock options weren't so lucrative.
3) Chris realized that the leader shapes the environment. The leader's vision had to be understood. The competencies to make the vision a reality must be clearly enunciated and acted upon.
4) The management group appeared to clone one another. Therefore, there appeared to be harmony and mature development. However, they were entranced in their own world of group think (the phenomenon that

occurs when groups can no longer do creative problem solving.)

Chris' coach suggested that an assessment be done to gain a better understanding of the group dynamics. She used a thinking styles instrument that has its genesis in brain dominance research to help Chris and the group gain an understanding of their own thinking styles. Wow, what an eye opener!

A lot has been written and continues to be researched on personality and psychological instruments. Some seem to make so much sense, while others appear fragmented and can only hold meaning for a Ph.D. The most meaningful instruments have a basis in sound research and can be communicated in a clear, crisp manner. Furthermore, a meaningful instrument can be used to help individuals and groups understand their level of effectiveness. They shouldn't categorize individuals into either/or outcomes; rather they should demonstrate the degree to which one leans in a certain dimension. As human beings, we are all composites of many components of thought, habit, character, emotion, and intellect. To state that any one component drives success is inaccurate. Rather, it is best to gain an understanding of an individual's thought patterns in order to understand how one can make the most of the whole. Through this understanding one can gain valuable knowledge of how groups work effectively.

Back to our new friend and CEO, Chris. He learned that there are four general thinking preferences of which we are all a part. An individual uses all four thinking styles but usually has two primary thinking preferences. One of those primary preferences usually prevails. In addition, there are secondary preferences – those in which one is comfortable operating. In some cases, individuals have tertiary preferences, which can mean avoidance to some methods of thinking or behavior.

The four areas of preference are:

1) logical/technical
2) organized/structured
3) emotional/feelings
4) conceptual/creative

Chris found that he leaned toward the conceptual/creative area and the emotional/feelings quadrant. These preferences enabled him to be a very strategic, people oriented leader. He knew that he could manage the analysis required to develop a strategy, but he opted to have those with a stronger penchant for analyses do that work. Likewise, Chris realized that he did not require a strong structure, did not require information in a linear fashion, and that he was willing to risk making decisions without all of the necessary data. Thus, his profile demonstrated a primary preference for *concepts* and *people* with secondary preferences for *logic/analysis* and *organization*.

Once Chris gained a better understanding of these preferences he knew it would prove valuable for his entire team. With his strong people orientation, he wanted to give the team a chance and did not relish the thought of firing even one of them. He wanted to give it his all before he made any structural decisions. In fact, he anticipated that the results of the profile might enable him to place some executives into positions that would build on their strengths.

Of course, there was the issue of the team's readiness for their new boss' ideas. He knew he could just push this profile on them, but he also realized that the best outcome of any organizational change effort required the group to be ready to learn more about themselves. He used his coach to facilitate an afternoon of the "here and now." Hindsight told him that she was effective in her approach. Her easy conversational style combined with a tight agenda of the here and now helped pave the way for a willingness to participate in the profile. In addition, she suggested one other thing to Chris... guarantee these executives that regardless of the outcome of the profiles, they would have jobs for the next twelve months. Besides, the data presented on the financial performance and market share of the company could have them all looking for jobs if something did not change. It wasn't the coach's brilliant approach that was the magic ingredient. Sure, she did a great job, however, it was Chris' own self-awareness that he needed a professional coach and facilitator that was the magic. As CEO he was tempted to take control, be the traditional leader, and force everyone to go his way. His own wisdom and ability to listen to his coach in other settings offered him this great alternative.

During the session, the coach developed three simple but major questions that the group should answer to improve the major components of company performance:

- What should they *continue* doing
- What must they *start* doing
- What must they *stop* immediately

Through these simple questions she was able to determine accurately the group's thinking preferences. She facilitated discussion about the continue, stop, start technique when those issues were in conflict with one another. And she was able to move them to an action orientation that would enable them to work in a common direction with a sense of urgency that was required for the tough times ahead.

After the "here and now" session, the group agreed that an awareness raising profile would be welcome. Chris' coach also believed that the group could embrace the work that would follow.

As it turned out, the profiles provided validation of the coach's own observations. However, the profiles provided each group member with credible results backed by solid research on the profile itself.

So what did these results reveal?

Of the seven direct reports, four executives had primary preferences for organization and structure. In fact, those four executives had strong financial management backgrounds.

Two others had strong preferences for logic and technical analysis. Of those two, one also had a strong but slightly lower preference for emotions and feelings. The remaining executive had a strong preference for conceptual thinking with an equally strong preference for organization and structure. As a result she was often thinking about ideas, but her need for structure kept her from taking the risk to bring these ideas into real strategy. She was an excellent candidate for some professional coaching.

The group found that they lived too much in the maintenance/stabilizing environment. While it suited their preferences pretty well, they had not learned how to adapt to their environment as business always dictates.

It was not a surprise that the group was uncomfortable and frightened with their new CEO. He was an idea person with the confidence, intuition, and ability to put a strategy together to turn the company around. Feedback revealed that they thought he was a little glib and may not be taken seriously in their culture.

A deeper look at thinking styles preferences

By learning the characteristics of each thinking preference, the group was able to work together more effectively, and the CEO was able to build success based on their strengths. Let's take a peek at how these characteristics play out:

The Logical/Technical thinker is factual, analytical, quantitative, and rational. These thinkers are achievement oriented and performance-driven. An example of this type of thinker is Star Trek's Mr. Spock. Individuals with a preference in this style want facts. They want to see critical analysis and usually prefer to deal with reality and the present rather than future possibilities. [1]

The Organized/Structured thinker is controlled, planned, conservative, detailed, and disciplined. They like to communicate in production oriented and task driven terms. Order and simplification are paramount to any undertaking.

Often you will hear someone with this preference say, "we have always done it that way", or "play it safe." Edgar Hoover, former Director of the FBI, exemplifies this thinking style. [2] These individuals can be perceived as domineering, small minded, boring, insensitive, and anti-social. [3]

Let's turn to our Emotional and Feeling friends. These thinkers can be perceived as the most sensitive and receptive. They are sensory, kinesthetic, interpersonal and symbolic. They need to be communicated to with feeling and consideration. Concerned with reality the same as the logical/ technical thinker, however, their reality consists not of words but of emotions. Experience is reality. It behooves any good leader to understand the importance of this thinking style. Appeal to feelings and senses is tied strongly to emotional branding. Manufacturers have long attempted to forge emotional links to their products. What is different today is that emotion is now the nerve center for nearly all product and service marketing. Reams of data show that the most effective way to forge meaningful bonds with customers is through their senses – an approach that is not being used enough.[4] Music is another sensory pathway for emotional branding. Gap, Toys "R" Us, and Eddie Bauer handpick songs they pipe into stores to emphasize brand positioning.[5] There are many opportunities to capitalize on this thinking style within the work environment itself. Those schooled strictly in number crunching and dense data can miss important opportunities if they discount this component of thinking.

A close cousin to our emotional/feelings thinker is the Conceptual/Creative thinker. Individuals with a strong preference in conceptual thinking thrive on the excitement of new ideas, possibilities, and questions that sound obvious but go to the heart of the matter. These thinkers are true visionaries. The down side to having a strong conceptual preference without other strong traits is that these individuals cannot usually be counted on to meet deadlines.

What this profile data means to leaders and coaches

There are many ways to dissect issues and strategize for success. When an individual or group is given the opportunity to work with a professional coach, it is essential for the coach to gain an understanding of the collective gifts that one brings to the work world. Equally important is the coach's ability to help others find that deep inner understanding of self that can make dreams become true reality. Through the use of an objective profile, a coach can help individuals unveil their own strengths, their own truths, and their own dreams.

Not all profiles are created equal; therefore, it is essential that the coach have a solid understanding of working with the strengths and weaknesses of any profile. Paramount to any instrument, however, the coach must be well versed in organizational issues, leadership styles, and the array of characteristics and gifts that make everyone unique.

A final word on Chris: Twelve months later, the company has made solid progress on improving employee turnover and the product development lifecycle. Profits are returning. Their turnaround is beginning, but it is taking longer to regain market share of some newer services. The company waited too long to put Chris in place as the new CEO, but things are on the right track. Three of the seven executives have been reassigned to positions that match their strengths. Chris is working with a great team that brings all thinking preferences to the table. The coach is doing very well as she has been able to utilize her organizational development expertise in the turnaround, and she continues to fulfill her dreams with other clients progressive enough to see the value in professional coaching.

Thinking styles exercise

Following is an abbreviated Thinking Styles Exercise that will give you a preliminary explanation of your own thinking style.

This exercise contains four sets of dichotic word pairs. For each set, review the five pairs on the basis of your general preferences for one or the other. Indicate your degree of preference for each of the two by dividing 10 points between them.

Example:

A – D Dichotic Pairs

Logical   3   -   Abstract   7
Be sure to allocate a total of ten (10) points between each set of pairs. Try not to assign a 5/5 split as you should normally lean more or less than half in each of the pairs.

After completing all four sets of five pairs each (20 total pairs), add up the scores.
The total of all four columns must add up to 200 points. The letter with the highest points indicates your primary thinking style.

If you have scores in two columns that are within five points of each other, they are considered equal levels of preference for purposes of this exercise.

A	B	C	D
___Analytical ___Argument ___Rational ___Explicit ___Logical			___Big Picture ___Experience ___Intuitive ___Unspoken ___Hasty
	___Verifies ___Controlled ___Procedural ___Organization ___Sequential	___Feels ___Emotional ___Free Form ___Relationships ___Harmonious	

A	B	C	D
___Informational ___Intellectual ___Objective ___Words ___Rational		___Interpersonal ___Sensuous ___Subjective ___Music ___Emotional	
	___Sequential ___Literal ___Disciplined ___Execution ___Planned		___Flexible ___Approximate ___Playful ___Conception ___Impulsive
___Total A	___Total B	___Total C	___Total D

Explanation of thinking styles

A – Logical/Technical Preference – Descriptors are factual, analytical, quantitative and rational.
B - Organized/Structured Preference – Descriptors are controlled, planned, conservative, detailed, and disciplined.
C - Emotional/Feeling – Those in this category would tend to be sensory, kinesthetic, interpersonal, and symbolic.
D - Conceptual/Creative - Thinking styles for this category include idea generation, visionary, abstract, seeing possibilities, imaginative.

About Diane Allen

Diane Allen, founder of *Encore Business Coaching,* is a professional Business Coach. She has over twenty years corporate experience and has served in senior level leadership positions in management, coaching, training, and human resources. She teaches on the undergraduate and graduate level at several colleges and universities. She is a member of the Board of Directors of two national corporations, a member of the Business Advisory Board of Rosemont College in Rosemont, Pennsylvania, and an arbitrator for the Dispute Resolution Board of Ford Motor Company.

Her education includes a Bachelor of Science in Business Administration, and a Master of Science in Training and Organization Development.

Diane's professional affiliations include membership in the International Coach Federation, Philadelphia Area Coaches Alliance, American Society of Training and Development, and the Society for Human Resource Management.

Her coaching practice includes working with growing businesses and clients in executive, management, and entrepreneurial roles, and with those aspiring to enhance their business and professional and life skills. Her work includes coaching in all aspects of business including leadership, communications, goal setting, strategic planning, public speaking and presentation skills, and achieving workable work-life balance. Diane believes that it is essential to incorporate good levels of fun and play into one's personal and professional life. As a trainer, Diane incorporates the use of music as a learning tool in her programs. She is certified in the HBDI, a thinking styles inventory. This complete version of the Thinking Styles Inventory identifies one's primary, secondary, and tertiary styles of thinking. It is also offered as part of customized training programs such as leadership, effective communication, group dynamics, and team building. The full program also includes working with a coach and performing activities that more fully develop all thinking styles.

Diane is pleased to offer a complimentary 30 minute coaching session to help individuals begin to discover their inner talent, vision, and personal action plan for a successful future.

She may be contacted at:

Encore Business Coaching
205 Ramblewood Parkway
Mount Laurel, New Jersey, 08054
email: dallen@encorecoaching.com
telephone: (856) 866-9990
toll free: (877) 533-9990

---

[1] Creative Problem Solving, Lumsdaine and Lumsdaine
[2] Creative Problem Solving
[3] The Creative Brain by Ned Herrmann
[4] Impressions Magazine, a Forbes Special Interest Publication, Issue 5/2001, I Second that Emotion
[5] Impressions Magazine, a Forbes Special Interest Publication, Issue 5/2001, I Second that Emotion

7

The Business of Relationships

By Michael R. Goldstein, CPA, MCC

B y the time I reached my forty-sixth birthday, I was convinced that I knew what life was all about. I knew all there was to know about running a business, even though I wasn't nearly as successful as many others I was aware of, and I knew how to handle employees, vendors, peers, and customers. Frankly, I knew how to deal with everyone. I knew just about everything!

I was also certain that the way I conducted myself at work was not the same way I behaved at home. After all, my business and personal lives were very different. I was quite capable of leaving my personal life behind when I left for the office, and of leaving my business life at work when I went home.

Does all this sound familiar? If it does, please pay careful attention, for I have both good and bad news to share with you. The bad news is that you probably don't see yourself the way you really are. You probably don't have a clue what others truly think of you. You don't realize the impact you have on people, and most likely, you are not consciously aware of how you react to others. What I have learned is that you can't really have good relationships with anyone else unless you first have one with yourself.

The good news is that you, and only you, are accountable for where you are in your life, and you have the ultimate power to change it. You create your own results and are singly responsible for what you do have and what you don't have. You are the only one who can do anything about it. In order for anything to change, however, you have to want it to change. If you do, you need only to seek the guidance you require. Remember, you are not a victim of the world around you. You are in control.

I was lucky. There was someone in my life who suggested these very possibilities to me and helped get me thinking. While I knew at a deeper level that things were not the way I wanted them to be, I was not yet willing to admit that to myself, or anyone else. She suggested that I attend an upcoming workshop that was focused on this very issue, the conscious versus the unconscious. Carolyn, who would later become my wife, and to whom I am eternally grateful, noticed that my words and my actions were incongruous. She could see me in a way that I could not. She believed that the experience of this workshop might benefit my life, and she was right. It would turn out to be the catalyst for the biggest, best, and most dramatic changes in my life.

This workshop experience helped me see that I had become numb to my very existence. I was rarely engaged in the moment. I had truly become an observer of my life rather than a participant in it. I had dismissed feeling my feelings, and I no longer recognized when I was hurt or angry; feeling loss or feeling joy. I was emotionally anaesthetized. Without consciously realizing it, I had made the decision that I was not going to be in "true relationships" with the people in my life, and it showed.

That was over ten years ago, and I can still remember how sick I felt when I first realized I had reached this stage in my life. I had a hard time remembering the details about my life; events from my childhood, my school days, and even my experiences as a young adult raising a family. This was the first time in my life I could recall feeling such utter loneliness.

The realization that I could not remember the details of these years, now gone and lost forever, was painful.

As terrible as I felt at that moment, that sick feeling also inspired me. It moved me to make a commitment to change my life, to correct as much of the past as possible, and to live the rest of it as fully as I could. I knew then that life was all about relationships; the relationships I had, and those I did not. As I worked hard to create new relationships, I discovered that what had to change first was the relationship I had with myself. Then, when that relationship changed, so did the relationships I had with everyone around me, both personal and business. The more I paid attention to how I was doing in my own life, the less I had to worry about the results.

There came a day when I made an agreement with myself. The only work I wanted to do was to assist organizations and individuals create relationships in their lives that would help them develop accountability, growth, positive working and living environments, and balance. It had become clear to me that wherever we are, at home, at work, or on the golf course, the key to success is in our relationships. The degree of that success is directly proportionate to the quality of those relationships. We do not shed any part of ourselves at the door when we leave for work, nor do we part with ourselves when we leave for home. We are who we are. RELATIONSHIPS ARE THE BUILDING BLOCKS OF EVERYTHING IN OUR LIVES. PERSONAL GROWTH, SELF ASSESSMENT, AND ACCOUNTABILITY ARE THE TOOLS WE NEED TO BUILD THESE BLOCKS .

For me, the challenge has been in bringing this philosophy into the lives of others, especially into the work place. Why is it so hard for people to take the first step? They tell me things are fine just the way they are. People seem to think that making changes (which I see as improvements), is an admission that something is "wrong" with them. The only thing that is wrong is that they are stuck. Stuck because of their fear. The fear of what might come next. The unknown. "If I begin to change, maybe things will get worse. Right now

I know what I am, I know what I have, and I know how to deal with it," they think. The message seems to be "I am safe".

When a company hires me to work with them, I am often disappointed when senior management does not participate in our workshops. Corporate executives tell me "my staff need this training", but rarely do they see any necessity for training for themselves. Ironically, a great deal of time is usually invested in talking about these executives, the problems that staff have with them, and the costs related to the lack of relationship between the two.

It's usually because of our fears that we avoid things, and we won't join in because we don't want to be seen as weak, emotional, or appear out of control. It took a crisis, even a series of crises, to wake me up. This is not uncommon. Someone has a heart attack, develops a life threatening illness, loses a job he's had for twenty or thirty years, or is overlooked for the promotion she was in line for. These kinds of things help give us instant clarity about where our important priorities have been sacrificed, or where we have compromised our values. Nothing less could have inspired us to change, or given us a deeper awareness of ourselves. That was also true for me. In the late 1980's, I experienced a business disaster along with personal life failures simultaneously. (I was in such a state of denial, I guess I needed a double whammy. Life, I have learned, will generously give you what you need, over and over again, until you get it - if that's what it takes!)

As I work with my clients, I see in them so much that they do not see in themselves, just as Carolyn and others had seen things in me that I did not. I chose to take the risk and be accountable for my life, whatever was good about it and whatever was not. So many of us will not take that risk. What is it that holds us back from taking this step? Why is it that corporate executives often tell me "my staff need training", yet won't participate themselves? Why do entrepreneurs, who are struggling, resist making changes? Why do we give ourselves seemingly logical "reasons" why we are not successful, let ourselves down, and break our commitments and promises?

The single most frequent comment I get from managers and supervisors is that they are frustrated with training. They go and learn, and even get excited about their training experiences, and then return to work inspired, only to be deflated by their bosses who respond to them, "Oh, forget about that or I don't know what you're talking about or I don't agree with that idea, just go and do it the way we've always done it". The first time this happens it's upsetting; the second time it's resented; and after that it becomes an "inside" joke around the water cooler.

Most managers and supervisors are aware of this problem. So are most company non-management staff. So what's the matter with senior management? I believe that some executives are aware of the need. I believe that many others are not. They are at the same level that I was at on my forty-sixth birthday. As I watch the evolution of business, and society itself, I am acutely aware of the increase in the importance of the individual's needs, and the lack of awareness and skills our leaders have to deal with this phenomenon. So much in our world is changing to serve the needs of people first, things that would have been taboo even five years ago, e.g., flexible work schedules, day care, family leave, maternity leave for both moms and dads, and telecommuting.

What will it take for you? Most people are just plain over protective of themselves; too worried about the images they have created. They refuse to put themselves in positions where they may be seen as "not" the person they have created. What's funny about this is that most of us are seen by others more accurately than we see ourselves. We attempt to hold on to some kind of fantasy about ourselves, not for the sake of others, although that's our rationale. We have decided what we must look like, sound like, and feel like based on our own private ideals, and we rarely, if ever, confirm this with others. We don't ask and no one tells us. Why? Because we don't want to know, and for the most part, there is no mechanism in place to help wake us up. There are no schools that will provide the education or the skills we need to develop or maintain intimate, productive relationships.

Dealing with the idea that we may have behavioral issues is akin to suggesting to people that they might be alcoholics. A behavioral pattern is very much like any addiction, but before dealing with it, one must first recognize there is a problem. Most of us are blind to the consequences of our behavior and our fears in much the same way that alcoholics are blind about their dependency. There is no hope of improvement until we admit the problem exists. For many, acknowledging that they would like to make some changes is like saying, "there's something wrong with me". People don't like to say that. It's a frightening reality for most of us, so we avoid making that statement, and we refuse to believe that things could be better. We would rather continue patterns that do not work than risk something new, the outcome of which is uncertain. The fear of the unknown rules.

I have seen this reaction consistently in my workshops. I am proud of my affiliation with the Police Academy where I do workshops on leadership. A big part of this leadership training is to work on the inner self. Most of the officers involved have become immune to their feelings as a result of what they experience daily on their jobs, and also because of the para-military nature of police departments. "Things are great, why would I want to do anything to change that?" They think they are unique, and yet, as we work through their many layers of resistance, those who do take the *risk* begin to reconnect to themselves, their compassion, caring, and enthusiasm. They start to remember why they became cops in the first place.

Resistance is not reserved for police officers. We all have ways that we use to avoid "playing the game". Some people make the whole idea of "personal growth" unimportant. Others are too busy to question their lives: "I won't have a chance to think about anything like this until after the children get married". Or they are righteous about it: "I'm sorry, that is okay for other people, but I don't need to change". People don't see how they have placed limitations on themselves or how stuck they are. We all stay where we are when we stop learning. This is true whether we are talking about a lawyer who stops reading the law, an accountant who no longer studies taxes, or a doctor who is not up to date with new medicines or procedures. The same thing applies to you and me. When we stop learning about ourselves, we become stuck.

So, without a crisis, why would someone voluntarily seek to make personal change? How can we convince anyone that more will become available to them through personal growth and self assessment, or that life really is about the relationships we have and our ability to create and nurture them? How do we make the point that this is important? After all, most people are comfortable with their lives, therefore, why should they mess with it? In my experience, most people will choose not to take the risk. Instead, they ask me to prove to them that there is a value to the risk. When I first started, I tried exactly that - to prove it to them; something which I could rarely do. Then I took a closer look at it. Why was I trying to prove to them that they can have better, happier, and fuller lives by learning how to build quality relationships?

The fact was that I couldn't prove it to them. But I am equally sure that no one could have proven it to me either. I had to *want* it. I had to be honest with myself first. Were things the way I wanted them to be? Not nearly. Was I willing to see myself as the problem, or did I want to blame other people or circumstances? Could I admit that I wasn't functioning at my best? And what about you? Are you where you want to be? Are you at your best? So many of us just can't acknowledge that there may be room for improvement. Some, who may even suspect that their lives are not exactly the way they would like them to be, are still unwilling to do anything about it.

I received a call from the HR department of a large, international corporation several months ago. They had invested a lot of time and money in hiring someone to head up one of their important departments. This person was more than skilled in the technical stuff, knew the job, and was successful in helping her employer achieve the goals they had set for this department. There was one problem though, many of the staff members had become disgruntled and left, and others were constantly complaining about being treated poorly. The company wanted me to work with her to try to change the situation.

In my initial meeting with her, I asked if she was aware that others were having a problem working with her. She acknowledged that there was a problem. I asked if she was interested in changing things. She was, but at the same time, she believed the problem lay with her staff and not with herself. She knew her superiors were concerned, and she saw her position as somewhat tenuous. However, because of the feedback she received from the behavioral assessment we prepared, and the conversations she had, at my request, with several of her staff, she began to acknowledge that staff members did have legitimate issues with her, and she was willing to make the attempt to change them.

This willingness to look at herself enabled her to make some dramatic changes to her relationships; changes that created better results and a more inspiring work environment. She is now happier and takes better care of herself. She has also found that because of her new self awareness and the changes that she made, she has become a better mom, wife, and friend. This makes her more cheerful and a lot more fun to be around. By making a change in one area of her life, she also changed other areas. Fortunately, her company took the initiative. What if that company had just decided to let her go? Usually that's what happens in most companies and for most of us.

I worked with a gentleman once who was on his third major management position in ten years. Once again, he was being overlooked for a promotion he firmly believed he had earned. The only problem was that his staff didn't want to work for him, and his peers had a difficult time working with him too. The same thing had happened at his two previous employers, yet once again, he believed that corporate politics was to blame for his failure.

Jack Welch, of GE fame, said, "An organization that develops on the outside faster than it does on the inside is doomed". I believe that is true, and furthermore, I think it's true for you and me as well. If we develop our outer behavior (persona) faster than our inner selves, we will not be able to create the kind of relationships that will serve to improve and enrich our lives. To whatever extent our lives are not exactly as we would like, or as we envisioned, then why not be honest about it? Why deceive ourselves into thinking that everything is okay?

I believe we all fit that description to one degree or another. I do, however, also know a few people who are working towards "having it all". They do know that they'll never really have it all, nevertheless, they are the joyous ones, always growing, always excited, and always passionate about their lives. They're fun to be around and have an energy which is magnetic. It's this burst of life they exhibit that seems to keep them young and vibrant. They just love being alive. They are the successful ones. They love being in relationships with others, and others love being in relationships with them. And they have honest, real, and loving relationships with themselves.

You can be one of them. With the proper guidance, support, commitment to the truth about reality, and a strong desire, anything is possible. And most of all, you deserve it!

About Michael R. Goldstein

Michael R. Goldstein, CPA, MA, MCC has been a professional and business consultant for more than thirty five years. He is the President and Founder of The Lincoln Management Group and the developer of COACH2000. The firm provides professional, personal and business consulting services, sales, management and leadership training, coaching and team building programs to its clients. The company's client and student list includes individuals and organizations from health care, education, finance, accounting, law, law enforcement, retail, manufacturing, insurance, real estate, public utilities and the media. Michael also maintains a private coaching practice.

Michael has played an integral role in assisting clients in reaching their goals. He has a solid record in guiding clients to developing leaders and building successful work and innovation teams. He also helps his clients in developing and implementing coaching and mentoring programs and to improve communications and feedback systems. His training and coaching programs help companies deal successfully with conflict and stress in the workplace and to develop positive attitudes creating healthy environments. Michael's emphasis on the importance of personal relationships and accountability helps his clients create successful customer service operations, spark immediate increases in performance and results, and successfully train and motivate managers, sales teams, work teams and entire staffs. His workshops concentrate on the knowledge, skills, techniques and processes necessary for the learning to be self sustaining over the long term.

He is a member of the faculty of Bryant College Executive Development Center and is the author and instructor of the leadership modules for the Rhode Island Municipal Police Academy and Emerging Leader certificate programs at the college. In addition to his Bryant affiliation he also teaches at the Graduate School of Johnson & Wales University and is an accredited instructor for continuing education with the Rhode Island Association of Realtors and the Rhode Island Society of Certified Public Accountants. Michael is also an instructor for the Rhode Island Manufacturers Partnership. He has been nominated to Who's Who in the World, in Society, in the East, in Rhode Island and is also named in Men of Achievement and the Nationwide Register of Executives.

Michael is a qualified trainer and seminar conductor for the Carlson Learning Company and the Performax Learning Network. He has served on the Board Of Directors of the Personal & Professional Coaches Association and is a member of the International Coaches Federation and holds the designation of Master Certified Coach. He has extensive training and experience working with groups and is a workshop conductor for Synergy Associates, Inc. Michael is a member of the Diversity Training Teams for the State of Connecticut Employees and the State Education Department. He has been a pioneer in the use of coaching in businesses, education and for individuals and families.

Michael is a published author having had a number of articles published. He has been a guest on a number of radio shows and has been interviewed by several newspapers. He was a presenter at the 5th International Conference of the International Coaches Federation. Michael is also a consultant with the International Business Team of the Rhode Island Export Assistance Center at the John H. Chafee Center for International Business at Bryant College.

He knows how to build and maintain productive processes through the development of personal skills. Because of his high energy and inspirational messages, he is frequently asked to speak at meetings and conventions. Participants describe his presentations as impactful and life changing. Michael's mastery at involving everyone in the process and his wonderful sense of humor make his programs enjoyable as well as educational.

8

Employing the Rewards of Childhood Management

by Robert M. Tierney

"Where is it?" came an exasperated, muffled yell from a room somewhere upstairs.

"Where's what?" I yelled back, hoping to overcome the barrier of wood and plaster.

"The business article that gave great ideas on how to handle employees," my wife replied as she walked down the stairs, all the while focusing on the watch she was attempting to strap to her wrist. "I spend hundreds of dollars for these business magazine subscriptions, just waiting for an article to appear on how to motivate the people I work with. Then finally, when one is written, I go and lose it!"

"I know that I am your husband, but I have been keeping a secret from you."

"Oh, I already know what you got me for my birthday ..." she grinned.

"No, that's not it," I said. "What every business consultant knows and charges you big money for, is ...", I hesitated for dramatic effect, "the best source for articles on how to manage and motivate employees is parenting magazines!"

"No way!" she exclaimed. "But all those business journals I get quote serious studies and get professorial Ph.D. people to write them."

"Yes, I know, but you get the same thing from parenting magazines, only cheaper."

"You can't compare what children do with how employees act!" she countered.

"Maybe," I conceded. "But would it be safe to say that the five things all children want in their lives are love, consistency, the need for achievement, recognition by others, and rewards for those achievements?"

"Well, maybe..." she said cautiously.

"The amazing part is that these things are exactly what employees are looking for too when they go to work! The trouble is that most managers believe the business myth that their employees gave up those needs before they started working for the company. As a result, the search for that special, magical, and different motivational technique leads managers through a forest of consultants, who recite their own brand of product incantations as the cure for the problem of the month.

"Every employee craves to know that when they show up to work, their supervisor appreciates their efforts and unique creativity; the rules and work expectations exhibit a consistency that can be trusted; there is ample opportunity to show creativity in their job; and recognition is given for the daily struggles and celebrations, even when small goals are met.

"We cringe at the heartlessness of parents who don't respond to these cues, but nod in understanding when a supervisor refuses to say thank you because "the employee didn't do anything special – he was only doing what was expected of him anyway!"

"That makes sense," my wife agreed, "but are you trying to tell me that we should treat our employees like children?"

"If that helps you to see your employees differently, then yes. What I am really trying to say is that even though we have grown up to be adults, we are still carrying around the same emotional needs that we had as children. And because we have the same timeless and universal cravings, the answers on how to meet those needs can still be found in the monthly parenting magazines. Wherever you read the word 'child', just replace it with 'employee'."

To test my theory, Miss-Doubting-Thomas dug out an old child-rearing issue and read off the teaser titles," 'How To Stop Your Child's Tantrums' ... How To Stop Your *Employee's* Tantrums. 'How to Raise A Caring Child' ... How To Raise A Caring *Employee*. I see what you mean now. I guess I need to catch up on my reading!"

"I'm curious as to the reason why you're spending your time with this stuff when you are usually busy with other projects," I wondered.

"We've been having trouble with our employee retention and motivation programs," she explained. "They start off with a splash, then everyone loses interest in them, and we're back to wondering why it's not working."

"Oh, so your company practices CMM."

"CMM? What's that?" she asked quizzically.

"Country Music Management! Country music singers divide relationships into two distinct management styles. The first is: 'I gotta do something special to win back your love.' In this style, good intentions are replaced with actions that are 'too little, too late'. Finally, when the Special One gets ready to say 'I quit', that's when panic sets in and the flowers are sent. This is the thinking behind retention programs that offer flash prizes and retention bonuses.

"The second style is gentle and very time-consuming. The lyrics to this type of song reflect the joy of someone who loves it when a partner consistently 'does the little things to keep my love'. And it's the little things that will keep an employee devoted to the relationship.

"Managers who consistently notice the talents of their staff, acknowledge it in ways that blend into the circumstances and become the most remarkable of memories that people will still recall years later."

"I understand now. Our company routinely performs the 'I gotta do something special' *song* and ends up losing people who would otherwise stay. But what do those parenting magazines say about this problem?" she challenged.

"The three C's." I winked.

"The three C's? What do you mean?"

"Any real estate agent knows that a successful home sale depends on 'location, location, location.' A similar rule exists for people-focused programs. A successful retention and motivation program needs consistency, consistency, consistency!

"I realize your staff appears uninterested; they're just not sure how to react. They have probably seen their managers make company policies and ignore them countless times. As soon as the rules seem to mean something, that's when the rules get changed. The employees have been expertly taught to expect a short-running campaign. So, why get excited about something that won't last long?

"Businesses have shortened their attention span to what can be accomplished *now*. The patience to wait until a plan comes together is not cost-effective. They have gone from strategic thinking to tactical acting.

"The problem is that Americans have a sense of time that is set to fast-forward. It's not uncommon for a CEO to demand a resolution in his employees' morale problem within 90 days. But it takes a minimum of 18 months for person-focused programs to begin showing positive results."

"Eighteen months! Don't the changes endure after a short class or program?" she asked.

"No," I shook my head. "As proof, look at the list of clients that a consultant proudly points to. Impressive company names like AT&T, Exxon, and American Express may be there. But these names are also on other consultants' client lists. Now, either these consultants acted as a tag-team, or the companies didn't follow through with the consultant's recommendations consistently."

"I have noticed that our company likes to bring in motivational speakers rather than teaching the staff those longer lasting techniques," she observed thoughtfully.

"Companies love to bring in motivational speakers to give pep talks to their employees during times of low morale. Even though the speaker can goose the employees to feel good about the company and their work during the brief event, once the celebrity leaves town, frustration and depression are likely to descend once again upon the workers. The company has spent a lot of money only to make the problem worse. Consistency is the only antidote."

"I can see what you are saying, but how do we do things differently?" she inquired.

"Develop a user-friendly environment," I replied.

"You mean everyone should smile more?"

"Not exactly." I countered. "Take a lesson from the Generation-X'ers. This is the first generation who grew up with instant feedback in the palm of their hands. Through the flamboyant graphics and video game controller, every mother's son and daughter receives between 70 to 100 external positive feedback responses per minute! But when they show up to work at your company, the positive feedback rate drops down precipitously.

"An exceptional manager can give about ten 'atta-boys' a day; the rest of the needed encouragement gets generated off the employee's own self-esteem battery. But what if that battery doesn't have enough juice to get through the week, or even the day?

"It's not personal when your employees say they want to do something different in their job. What they really mean is that they are not receiving enough external positive reinforcements from their current duties to maintain their interest or attention. Don't change their jobs - just train their managers on how to increase the frequency of positive feedback to each of their employees."

"This is great stuff," my wife smiled. "The part that is difficult for me though is having the time to be aware of everything people in my department are doing. What can I say that will make a difference?"

"It's not what you say, but the questions you ask," I told her.

"The most effective question to use is 'how did you do that?' Do you remember the feelings you had when I asked you about that inventive brush stroke you incorporated into the painting you were working on?"

"You weren't using psychology on me, were you?" she mocked playfully.

"Yes. . . but I was also very interested in hearing how you did it! The most wonderful thing I remember is that your eyes brightened immediately!"

"Yes, I remember that! I had a chance to show off the best parts of something I had created, and now, whenever I pass that picture in the hallway, I relive the thrill of making it and the interest you showed. I looked forward to attending another painting class," she added enthusiastically.

"Well, imagine how your employees would feel after you asked them, 'How did you do that?'"

"I get it now," she exclaimed. "Asking this question would solve two problems for me at once. The employees would have a chance to tell me what projects they are working on and allow them to celebrate their success all over again, and it would also give me a chance to offer external feedback for the good work they are doing. What else should we be doing?"

"Next," I started, "don't rely on your quarterly, motivational dinner programs to keep your top performers. These are the kinds of people who know their worth in the business world, and they won't wait around hoping that you will notice their best efforts. If you don't notice immediately, they will search out other companies and managers who will.

"They'll also notice how you treat them, and others, during the times between the motivational award dinners. You know, it is hard to celebrate at these dinners when you have been beat up during the rest of the year."

"You are so right. I do look back over the year and compare what my bosses are saying with how they treated me. Occasionally, I wonder what message they want me to pay attention to – the way they treated me during the year, or the words they're saying now," she pondered.

"We're back to the idea of needing consistency," I observed.

"I'm confused now. Is it, or is it not, possible to get people to feel good about their jobs?"

"It is simpler than you think," I replied. "You just have to follow a few simple rules. The first rule is to cut down on the number of rules you have. It's easier to make and enforce decisions when you have a policy manual the size of the Ten Commandments, rather than the IRS Tax Code! Your staff doesn't get confused, and you don't have to worry if the decision is fair enough for everyone.

"Rule Two – Be careful what you reinforce, because you are sure to get more of it. If you make it a point to reward on-time work attendance positively, your staff will make it happen. It's when you don't reward on-time behavior that you inadvertently begin to reward the idea that it is OK to come in late."

"But wouldn't a written reprimand give the same message?" she asked.

"Great question! That brings me to Rule Three – Only positive reinforcement brings out the best in people. Negative consequences never solve problems by themselves. The use of reprimands only serves to build anger and lower the motivation to cultivate the behavior you want to nurture."

"No wonder I get a further decrease in performance after I give someone a reprimand," she declared.

"Rule Four," I continued. "Managers who reinforce the smallest improvements achieve the fastest changes. Just as you like to break down your goals to achievable stepping stones, your staff likes to measure their improvements in the mastery of their new skills by your numerous 'atta-boys'. Although we can see the moon from our bedroom window, an astronaut has to make over 57 course corrections to land on that target."

"Now I understand how it can get so time consuming, but at the same time, it gives the employee a definite map to navigate from," she said. "Without that direction, it's easy to lose your way."

"Finally, Rule Five – Since you change people every day, make sure you change them for the better. We always leave an impression with the people we meet. Sometimes the things we do create a learning experience. Imagine the history of the world if the learning experiences that Adolf Hitler witnessed were different. How different would you be if your mentors saw each moment as sacred?"

"Wow, I never considered the depth of my influence on people. I do a lot of things that I don't think twice about," she said. "It sounds like you need to know what values you hold, before you can teach them."

"You are always revealing your values," I corrected. "To be aware of them helps you to decide how to teach them better. An added benefit of knowing your values is that it is easier to make your life decisions. During an interview, Gene Rodenberry revealed that the primary reason he incorporated the Prime Directive into the Star Trek scripts was to answer plot questions the other writers may have while developing their script continuity. Knowing and sticking to the show's Prime Directive made it easier to modify and enforce those characters' actions."

"I just knew your Trekkie trivia would pay off someday," she ribbed me.

"Now, Miss Know-It-All, what did you learn?" I quizzed.

"One, all my employee management tips can be found in the monthly parenting magazines," she began counting off. "Two, be consistent in the behavior I am looking for and rewarding. Three, give positive and frequent rewards for improvements to those goals, and four, be fully aware of my prime directives, since I am frequently teaching them to others!"

"Well done! That's correct," I rewarded. "These are the small, yet important things that any manager can do – no consultant needed. The most important point is that each of these actions must be performed consistently!"

"Boy, you just saved me a lot of money!"

"Don't worry, I'll send you my bill in the morning," I grinned.

"Good, that means I get to play Post Office tonight," she replied coyly.

About Bob Tierney

Bob Tierney is a Nationally Certified Counselor, hypnotherapist, and Certified Motivational Interpreter with over twenty years of clinical knowledge in mental health counseling. He obtained his Master's

counseling degree from Southern Illinois University and expertly employs his skills with Eye Movement Desensitization and Response (EMDR) to rapidly enhance the performance levels of his business clients.

Not only has Bob developed a growing list of private coaching clients, he also has a unique niche in teaching other coaching professionals on how to integrate assessments into their special style of coaching. He shares these skills by conducting college-credit courses to students and other Executive Coaches interested in effecting sweeping positive change in the organizations they work in. Bob co-developed the curriculum currently being taught in the Lancaster Chamber of Commerce Mentoring and Coaching Academy for supervisors and managers.

Bob's expertise has been highlighted in magazine and news articles on workplace motivation and mentoring. A partial publications list includes Central Penn Business Journal, Advance for Respiratory Therapists, and Business Management Summary.

He can be heard teaching teleclasses through the Comprehensive Coaching University, and be seen on the web at: http://www.voicenet.com/~rtierney and emailed through: rtierney@mac.com

Private coaching sessions can be arranged by calling his home office at (717) 560-4335.

9

Cultivating A Joyful Perspective

by Cheryl Bakke Martin

There is a children's story called "Jubal's Wish" by Audrey Wood. It is a wonderful story about a little bullfrog who is very happy. All is right in his world. He skips down the path on a bright, sunny day carrying a picnic basket, his feet hardly touching the ground. He delights in the blue sky and the singing birds, flowers surround him everywhere. He can hardly wait to share his picnic lunch with his friends. But when he meets his friends he finds they are miserable and complaining... about everything. There's too much work to do, the house is a mess, the toadlets are misbehaving, there are no more adventures, no one wants an old boat and an old sailor, no one is in the mood for a picnic... Jubal has one wish: he wishes his friends were as happy as he is.

What makes us look at the world differently, each one experiencing something unique from our own perspective? Do our circumstances determine how we see the world? Certainly that can have an impact, but it is not the determining factor in how we evaluate the situation. We choose how we will respond. There are many stories of individuals who have endured considerable hardship, yet in spite of that, chose to see the bright light, the deeper meaning in the situation.

95

Focusing on that tiny bright light is what often allowed them to triumph; it gave them something to live for, and to strive to create better circumstances for themselves.

Viktor Frankl, a psychiatrist who endured the tortuous experience of the internment camps at Auschwitz during the Second World War, developed an entire branch of therapy based on this very notion. He was trying to understand the psychology of life in prison and why and how it was that some people had the ability to survive these horrible conditions, while others did not. One would expect that one's physical strength and health would be the primary factor. During the nearly four years of his imprisonment he came to really understand the power of meaning and how directly it influenced our behaviors, happiness, and well being. Viktor shares in his book, "Man's Search for Meaning", the dreadful conditions they survived. He tells about having to march very early every morning for miles and miles in the bitter cold, wearing nothing but rags and only the remains of shoes, some with the toes cut away because they did not fit the feet of the wearer. Often their limbs were swollen with edema and blistered. If they were caught tearing pieces from their blankets to use on their feet to ease the pain, they were severely beaten, if not hanged for their "crime". Food consisted of a few ounces of bread and scarcely a quart of thin broth each day. Yet under these circumstances, a prisoner would rush to his comrades and ask for them to come and see the most wonderful sunset he'd ever witnessed.

> "...in the final analysis it becomes clear that the sort of person the prisoner became was the result of an inner decision, and not the result of camp influences alone."
> "...everything can be taken from a man but one thing: the last of the human freedoms – to choose one's attitude in any given set of circumstances, to choose one's own way."

Our ability to endure, survive, triumph over adversity, to see the beauty and joy in the moment, to see and learn the lessons in the challenges we face, is also what allows us to experience a life of happiness and joy.

Our evaluation of a situation often determines our experience. Many years ago I worked in an accounting office for a very large trucking company. The work was tedious and boring and there was an incredible amount of paper that had to be processed under tight deadlines. It wasn't work that I was particularly suited to, but I took on the challenge each day to see how fast I could work. I continued to look for new challenges and moved to new positions every opportunity I could. What was discouraging to me was the attitude of many of the people with whom I worked. They were miserable and seemed to delight in sharing that misery. There were daily complaints about everything, too little time, money, resources, office space, and too many invoices, bills, phone calls, demands... and on and on. The environment created was toxic. There were angry and disrespectful interactions among co-workers and even with customers on the phone. What was curious to me was that even though it was very apparent that most were incredibly unhappy, very few actually made any effort to change the situation or to leave to find something better. It was as if they enjoyed the misery and never wanted to leave. I, on the other hand, eventually left, and in my "retiring speech" I wished for each of them that they not allow themselves to be so complacent that they did not search out something different that would bring them enjoyment in their work. The Human Resources manager shot me a menacing look, but I left smiling. It was truly what I wished, that everyone there would be happy. If that meant leaving the company, then so be it. Despite the discouraging environment, I am grateful for my experience there. I learned many things about the work, about relationships, about behavior, and about myself and my abilities. In the end, my personal perspective allowed me to find the gems in an otherwise negative experience.

Do you ever wonder how two people can be in the exact same set of circumstances and see things so completely differently? It's that old glass half full / half empty thing. Take for instance two individuals driving in their vehicles. They get cut off by another driver. One responds by shrugging and laughing it off, careful to slow down and leave plenty of room between himself and the offending car, now in front of him. The other responds by swerving, swearing, shaking a fist, speeding up beside the offending vehicle and making gestures, and then trying to cut the other driver off. His heart is racing; adrenalin is pumping relentlessly through his veins. He arrives at his destination still enraged. Who do you think enjoyed his day? Which one was pleasurable to be with that day? Who do you think will live longer? And to think that all this comes down to a simple matter of choice. We all choose how we respond in any given situation. No one else can make us feel anything. We alone choose to respond with anger, or with compassion, or understanding, or laughter, or whatever. We choose. Knowing this gives us the power to change how we respond.

It does seem, however, that this propensity for seeing the good and for finding the joyful is easier for some than for others. The Nature vs. Nurture argument may be at play here. It could be who we are, and it could be what we have learned and experienced. This doesn't really matter. What does matter is that assuming the "glass half full perspective" has a profound effect on our ability to enjoy life. Not to mention that our health is better, our ability to rise to a challenge is improved, we are more apt to see an opportunity and have more courage to go after it, and we are just generally able to find beauty and fulfillment in each moment.

If this all seems a little "Pollyanna-ish" to you, it isn't. What it is, is childlike. If you watch a child you can see this perspective in action. Everything is as if it is a new experience. The joy and delight can be seen on their faces. They express their feelings with laughter and squealing. Or if they are sad, they cry. They see the "WOW" in everything. A bug is beautiful. The clouds are fun. The air smells good. A mud puddle or a pond to throw rocks into is an exceedingly good find. Are you feeling a little too grown up to behave like a child? Let me share with you one of my best days in my corporate career. One morning I drove in to the city and parked at the train station where I catch the train into down town. It was a fresh early spring morning and we were experiencing a late snowfall of huge, sticky snowflakes. It was peaceful walking down the path. I noticed all the cars rushing by and wondered if anyone else noticed how pretty the scene was this morning. The sun was just rising, sending a golden, pink glow over the sky, which was reflected back in the towering glass office buildings behind me. The thick, huge snowflakes were floating down like feathers. As I looked over the small open area next to the path, I realized that there was enough accumulation to make a snowman, and I smiled at the thought. Briefly, a small voice muttered, "Don't be ridiculous. You need to get to work and you are dressed in a business suit and coat. You'll be late and wet." Fortunately, my childlike voice beckoned louder. "Oh come on, what chance will you have to do this again? It's a glorious morning... this is what real life is about - enjoying the moments we are given." What the heck! I abandoned all adult reasoning and jumped into the snow. Rolling a ball around and watching it get bigger and bigger, the snow so sticky and wet. It was effortless and I was giggling. What would people think if they saw me? I felt like a little girl again. No worries, cheeks rosy, laughing, and having fun in the morning snow. My little snowman complete, standing beside the path, I thought he should be waving at whoever came down the path next so that they might experience some amusement at the sight. I found a few rocks to give him a face with a huge grin and branches to make him wave. I stomped off my boots and brushed off my coat, picked up my bag, and stood back to admire my handiwork, a huge smile across my face to match my snowman. I felt so silly and exhilarated. Truly this moment was a gift and I had seized it with the heart of a child. The train ride in was unbearable, for I could hardly keep from laughing out loud. I'm sure many of the people wondered why I had this ear-to-ear grin like the Cheshire cat. I felt so good, and I couldn't wait to get to the office to share my story. To this day, I have never experienced a better day at work.

For an adult to take on this childlike attitude is kind of like adopting a "Forrest Gump" mentality, really. If you have not seen that movie, pick it up at the video store, and thoughtfully take it in. Here is a man born with mental and physical challenges, yet who is able to live an extraordinary life. Why? Because he approaches it with the innocence of a child. He does not even hear the voices that say something is not possible. He believes in himself, in love, and in life. He accomplishes more than most will because he does not choose to be stuck, or to live by the limitations that others would try to impose upon him. He chooses to move forward. He sees the goodness in people. He delights in the small things like cutting the grass with a riding mower, sitting in a tree, and eating ice cream. He honors his friendships and is generous and giving. His glass is half full. And the universe responds back with many opportunities and blessings.

Does this mean that if your glass seems half empty to you that you are doomed to a life of unhappiness? Absolutely not. The power to choose our responses to life cannot be taken away from us. What it means is that we need some practice to learn a new way of seeing things. Old habits need to be let go and replaced with new habits and thought patterns that are positive and supportive. Working with a Personal Coach would definitely make the process easier and likely quicker. You can also solicit the support of those you love to help you take on a new life perspective and start with the steps outlined below.

1. Becoming aware

Notice what you notice. Start to pay attention to what grabs your attention. Do you gravitate to the stories about "what is wrong with…"Are you busy sharing negative information? We live in a time that seems infatuated with misfortune. Our media reports about accidents, deaths, crimes, our government parties complain bitterly about one another pointing fingers of blame at others, businesses are unsatisfied with multi million dollar profits. The popular television show of the day, Survivor, tells the story of individuals enduring hardships in the Australian outback. Do we focus on their achievements? No, the talk around the water cooler is centered around who will be the unfortunate one to be expelled next. So it is very easy to be sucked into a mentality that is focused on the negative. Just become aware of where your attention rests and what stance you take. For one whole day take note of your perspective without judgment. It took a long time to adopt this frame of mind. It will take practice to change it.

Some situations just naturally give rise to anger, grief, and self-pity. Stuffing your feelings is not healthy either. It is necessary to allow yourself time to express those feelings in a constructive way in order to be able to move on. Christopher Reeves, the actor who became a quadriplegic after a fall from a horse, says that he allows himself 10 minutes of self-pity each morning and that's it. It's over and he can get on with the rest of the day unhindered by feelings of negativity and disappointment. Allowing a time for the expression of grief, anger, disappointment, or any other depressing emotion is an essential step in purging ourselves of thoughts that keep us stuck.

2. Acceptance

We are all exactly where we need to be in our personal journey. When we are able to recognize that everything happens for a reason, we are able to begin to look for the lesson in any given situation. A few years ago, when my first son was born, I struggled with postpartum depression. One of the reasons I was able to overcome it in a relatively short period of time was the thought that I was experiencing this for a reason. There was something I needed to learn that I had not paid attention to earlier in my life. This struggle had a lesson for me, and when I found it, I would be able to grow. In that particular situation the lesson for me was about taking care of myself. I had become unrealistically demanding of myself and was not able to allow time for self-nurturing. My bout with depression forced me to slow down and learn how to do just that. My challenge was a gift, a lesson learned that I can now share with others. Many hardships are very difficult to understand, and some things seem to have absolutely no good reason for occurring. Certainly, when we are in the midst of a crisis it is not easy to understand "why." In time, and in looking back, the why becomes clearer. Even in death there can be a reason – another life is given hope, a cause is established, awareness is built, understanding grows. One of Victor Frankl's favorite quotes from Friedrich Nietzsche was, "He who has a why to live for can bear with almost any how". Suffice it to say that accepting where we are allows us to use the situation as a springboard for personal growth. There is a knowing that the divine is at work in our lives and that there is a purpose for everything and everyone we experience.

3. Examine our position

As you pay attention to your responses, look at what you have found and consider the following:

What are your opinions about yourself, about others, and about the world? Are they about hate or about love? Are they supportive or destructive? Do they uplift or tear down? Do they bring you closer to people, or do they keep you at a distance?

What are your expectations of yourself and others? Are they realistic and understanding? Do they allow for the learning that mistakes bring? Does perfectionism keep you from trying anything, getting things completed, or keep you in a state of self-disgust? Expectations need to keep us forging forward toward a dream and to help us keep on believing that we can achieve what we set our hearts on. If our expectations only serve to hold us to an unrealistic standard, they become destructive rather than supportive.

Do you compulsively make judgments? Is there a tendency to look something or someone over and make some kind of evaluation – too thin, not clean enough, conceited, bad hair day, dreadful parenting, lousy driver, terrible suit? We may even be looking in the mirror when this is going through our heads. Either way, this type of thinking serves no one. A quote of Wayne Dyer's that has stayed with me is: "True freedom is being free of the good opinion of others." Likewise, building understanding and acceptance of others means that we free ourselves and others of our good opinion. Examining the ways we respond and evaluate gives us the opportunity to choose differently if what we find is not supportive of ourselves and of those around us.

4. Reframe our point of view

All this examination keeps us focused on the present moment, which is helpful since the power to change lies in the present moment. We cannot change the past, and our only opportunity to impact positively on the future lies in what we choose to do today, and in each moment.

As you look at your answers to the above questions, ask yourself: What are the alternatives? How else could I respond? What is the other side of the story? Do I understand all the circumstances surrounding the actions or behavior of the other person? A story I have heard that illustrates this is about a man who is riding the train with his children. He is sitting quietly staring out the window, seemingly oblivious to the behavior of his children. They are being unruly, loud, and generally annoying to the other patrons of the train. He is doing nothing to discipline them or to get them to sit down. Watching this situation, we are sympathetic to the frustration of the people who are having to put up with these misbehaved children. One patron, who is increasingly irritated, makes the judgment that these are very bad children and that this is an irresponsible parent. It is only later when we truly understand this man's situation that we change from frustration to compassion. You see, this man explains to the aggravated patron that he is very sorry that he wasn't paying attention, and that his wife, the children's mother, had just died, and they were making their trip back home from the hospital. I hold this story in my memory and think of it whenever I am tempted to pass judgment on another's behavior. I cannot fully understand where they are at or what they are dealing with in their lives, so I am ill prepared to make an accurate assessment. It serves me only to remain understanding by simply not judging at all. Any evaluation that we are required to make then, must be done only when we completely understand all sides of the situation. Seek understanding first. Our expectations can serve us well if they are attainable and dynamic, changing as we grow and as our circumstances and values change. As well, our expectations are best kept for ourselves. If we have no expectations of others, we cannot be disappointed. We can certainly have discussions about what behavior is acceptable in any relationship, but we still do not have any real influence on how someone else chooses to behave in the end. Therefore, if we are holding someone else up to our expectations of them, we set ourselves up for disappointment should they not live up to our standards. Help them choose their own attainable expectations, if we are in a position of influence.

In any situation, what we choose to focus on has a direct impact on our experience. Now that you are aware of your natural opinions, attitudes, expectations, and judgments, you can choose to refocus if necessary. Look for the gems:

- The lessons to be learned as we work through a difficulty.
- The beauty that surrounds us – the colors in the sunrise and sunset, the opalescent green on a beetle's shell, the smells of the flowers, the stillness in the mountains or the countryside. If you don't have the opportunity to experience this where you live, give yourself the gift of a trip into nature to delight in the natural

From: Clarke 336 41

Thursday
→ Ask Wanda
→ Mail for Dinfren
→ Bills (telephone) AT&T

→ Am Grocenie
→ meatfish
→ diaper
→ Young Coconut juice

beauties there. Or buy flowers to enjoy in your home or office.

- The joy in the present moment. Take time to savor every experience. When you eat chocolate, buy the really good stuff, find a lovely spot to enjoy it, and relish every bite. Notice the texture on the roof of your mouth, lick every morsel off your finger, take your time, and enjoy! When with your children, get down on the ground and see things as they do. Let them take the lead and show you the wonder of things. Play games, get dirty, hug them lots, notice the softness of their skin and the smell of their hair. They are truly a gift, and we have much to learn from them if we will take the time and be completely present when we are with them.

- The things in our lives that we are grateful for, proud of, or have accomplished. Often we are swept away in thoughts of what is missing from our lives. If we give ourselves a chance to recognize what we already have, we begin to see that things really are pretty good. There is a tendency to overlook those accomplishments, skills, or talents we do have simply because they come so naturally to us and we don't think much of them. In relationships, the old adage holds true: we often don't know what we have until it's lost. Taking people, particularly those we love, and other blessings in our lives, for granted keeps us from fully enjoying them. Keeping a gratitude journal or simply making a ritual to spend the last waking moments of the day dwelling on what we are thankful for in our lives allows us to end the day positively and in appreciation for the day and its gifts. Beginning the day in the same way can be even more powerful, as it sets up how we approach the rest of the day.

- Even the mundane task can be a source of joy. Peeling potatoes can be a relaxing and meditative experience if we approach it that way, allowing ourselves the opportunity to turn off our heads for the moment and peacefully complete the task. Several years ago, my husband and I had the opportunity to travel to Japan. While we were there we visited many temples, shrines, and gardens. At one temple there were large forested grounds surrounding it. The garden was exquisite. Not a pebble or twig out of place. Even the moss that covered the ground was a pristine carpet of green. As we were about to leave, we noticed a woman on her knees working in the garden. She sat crouched in the moss, working diligently. As we got closer we could see just how she was going about her task. With a look of peaceful delight, she groomed the moss with a small set of what looked like tweezers! I was astounded. Surely this was a labor of love, an honor, and a quest of personal joy and peace. Had she approached her responsibility with disdain, each day would have been misery. This perspective would have left her in a position of despair. I learned in that moment that absolutely anything can be done with a heart of joy, if we only choose to pursue it that way.

In what ways can you reframe your experiences to look for, find, and experience the goodness in each encounter? Be aware that you are learning new thinking habits and know that this will become easier over time and with persistent practice. Post reminders around the house if this will help you make the shift. The mirror where you first look each morning is a great place for this.

5. Seek opportunities

When we can see the lessons we are offered in life and learn from them, we are able to grow and move forward. We can seek out new opportunities, and we are more apt to notice when a real opportunity stands before us. Know what is important to you in your life, where you want to go, what you need to change along the way, and create a vision. Make plans – the steps required for you to get to where you want to be. When an opportunity sits on your lap as you move toward your vision, seize it! You may still feel fearful and uncertain – go for it anyway. All of these things require focus, support, and a belief in your capabilities. I believe we really have no idea just how much we can accomplish, and we would astound ourselves if we completely lived up to our potential. I love Henry Ford's words: "If you think you can, or you think you can't, you're right!" It is true, anything is possible for those who believe. (And for those who forge ahead even on days when they have trouble believing.) A personal coach can be a tremendous support in helping you through this process. And there are several books written by coaches that can help to get you started.

6. Enjoy now

When we envision a brighter future for ourselves, we can sometimes forget that today and its pleasures are afoot. Life is about the journey, not about the destination. Goals and dreams give us something to work towards, but the present day remains the greatest gift. What we do with it and how we approach it is what makes life enjoyable. Be fully present in every activity and every personal encounter you experience each day. Try on the "eyes of a child" to find the wonder in this moment. My dad, a man with the heart of a child, has a saying that he shares with whoever will stand still long enough to hear it, and that is: "You're a long time dead!" That is his way of telling people that NOW is the time to take up that hobby you've always wanted to try; NOW is the time to jump on your motorcycle and take a trip to that place you've always wanted to visit; NOW is the time to get in the workshop and experience the pleasure of creativity; NOW is the time to enjoy your children before they grow up and move away. Plan for tomorrow, live today, savor this moment with the exuberance of a child…. carpe diem…with a thankful and joyous heart!

Jubal did get his wish, although not the way he expected. It came through an unexpected twist of fate, a struggle that he and his friends worked through and triumphed over together. Happiness was found in the midst of hardship, on the journey they found themselves on together, and on the adventure they chose to create and remain on today.

About Cheryl Bakke Martin

Cheryl Bakke Martin is a Personal and Professional Coach, Facilitator and Speaker. She is President of Inspirations Unlimited, a company she established to inspire others to define and actively reach for their goals and dreams, creating a successful lifestyle by design. She provides her clients with a safe and supportive atmosphere to experience the power of self-discovery, self-love, wellness, and personal effectiveness.

Cheryl spent the last half of her 15 years in the corporate environment, leading workshops and providing individual coaching in the area of career and life focus. She is formally trained in Adult Education, Career Development, and is currently completing her ICF Coaching designation. As a Certified Louise Hay Workshop Leader, she has been trained under the guidance of internationally recognized metaphysical counselor and teacher, Louise L. Hay. She is a member of Toastmasters International and the Canadian Association of Professional Speakers where she continues to hone her skills as a professional speaker.

She has created and delivers ongoing workshops in her pottery studio on "Rediscovering The Joy of Play", a class that re-ignites the creative and playful in the participants. Taking time for fun and personal wellness activities is a principle she lives by and encourages in her clients.

As a wife and mother of two young boys, she understands first hand how difficult it can be to juggle a career she is passionate about and a family she is committed to and loves dearly. To this end she is focused on seeking out the things that she finds truly enjoyable in life and on staying balanced, well and healthy. She aims to find and appreciate the beauty and joy in each moment and encourages her clients to reach a place in their lives where they, too, are experiencing true joy and personal fulfillment.

Committed to insuring the personal and professional success of her clients as they choose to define it, her lifestyle and philosophy is based on a firm belief in learning, combined with core values which demand personal excellence, wellness and a commitment to achievement and fun. Most importantly... she really cares about people. "My passion is to see my clients live the life they truly desire. It is a great privilege and honor to be able to witness their dreams come true."

For more information about Inspirations Unlimited, or to contact Cheryl, visit her website at:

www.inspirations.ab.ca

10

Inner Coaching

by Stacey and Valerie Hylen

"We cannot always control our thoughts, but we can control our words, and repetition impresses the subconscious, and we are then master of the situation."

FLORENCE SCOVEL SHINN

Where do you turn for the missing secrets to success? Which motivator holds the key? How many seminars do you need to attend? If you have read lots of books and studied the most common "secrets of success" and life still has not delivered all it can and should, you will be delighted and amazed, and probably surprised, at how simple the answer is. Most of these books have given you lots of good advice, and if you have followed it, chances are it has probably brought some level of control and improvement, but it probably has not been long lasting. The reason for this is that the motivation has been external.

In order to reach true and lasting success and achieve the extraordinary life you are capable of having, it is necessary to apply the success tools internally. Inner Coaching is a tool that will enable you to achieve your goals by being aware of your negative inner talk and consciously substituting positive inner talk. Whether you are aware of it or not, the inner talk that is constantly running through your head affects every area of your life. Where you are in your life right now is a direct result of your own inner talk.

As children we were told "NO" thousands of times. We were told we were silly, stupid, not capable of certain things, and we mostly accepted this as true. Society feeds on the bad news that is fed to it. The general attitude that prevails is WHO has it the worst? We talk on the phone, or get together and complain and try to outdo one another with stories of how bad our life, job, spouse, day is. Are you someone who thinks "that's a good idea but it won't work for me", brushes off compliments, is stuck in a rut, and thinks that success is for other people?

You are not the only one experiencing this negative inner talk. It is no coincidence that 75% of small businesses fail within five years and that up to 75% of what we say to ourselves about ourselves is negative and counter productive. What if from the time you were born you were only told positive things about your capabilities? Can you think of a time you did have a "coach" who encouraged you and believed in you until you were successful at something? Most people learned to ride a bike when they were young, before the inner gremlins took over. Many of us who learned to ride a bike as a kid would not have attempted to learn as adults. What enabled us to learn when we kept falling down? Why didn't we quit? We probably had an encouraging "coach" supporting us until we could believe for ourselves that we could, actually, master this skill.

I remember my Dad running along beside me with one hand on the bike, encouraging me that I could do it. Even when I went into the hedges, he immediately put me right back on the bike telling me that he was positive that "you almost have it, try again, you can do it!" This is something that we can learn to tell ourselves. Would your life be different today?

Would you have set different goals? What would you love to do that you have told yourself is not possible?

Stop and listen to your inner talk right now. Are you thinking that's just the way I am; I have tried before and nothing works for me? Notice what you are thinking - that is your inner talk at work. Is your inner talk helping you or holding you back?

In order to understand how your Inner talk works and how to apply Inner Coaching, it is necessary to understand how your mind works. Your brain is divided into two distinct parts, the conscious mind and the subconscious mind. The conscious mind does the rational thinking and either accepts or rejects what is thought about as true or untrue.

The subconscious mind is subject to the input of the conscious mind. It accepts what the conscious mind tells it as true. It does not logically decide if something is true or false. The subconscious mind is the seat of emotions, intuition, and is the storehouse of memory. All the actions and results in your life are the results of the thoughts impressed on your subconscious mind. The subconscious mind creates results in your life based on what is fed to it by the conscious mind. Just like soil in a garden, your subconscious mind doesn't differentiate if the thoughts planted in it are good or bad, it just creates what is planted there. Whether you plant seeds that will produce weeds or flowers is your conscious decision to make. Research has shown that the brain operates like a computer, if you feed it negative input (programming), you will have negative results; if you feed it positive programming, you will have positive results.

> *"Man is what he thinks all day long."*
> Ralph Waldo Emerson

Following are several activities that will help you reprogram your subconscious mind for success. By training your subconscious mind it will respond more quickly to the requests you make of it. The first step in training your subconscious mind is self awareness. Work with a coach or team up with a buddy to tame the gremlins that have been keeping you from achieving all that is possible for you.

Activity #1 Start noticing your inner talk

Step 1: Tune in to your inner talk, you know, that inner critic that tells you that you aren't good enough, that brushes off compliments, and tells you to quit when faced with any obstacles.

Step 2: Take a small notebook and throughout the day jot down any negative inner talk you notice. You may be startled to notice how much negative inner talk you have. Tuning into your negative inner talk is like buying a new car - before you buy it you don't ever notice any on the road, but once you have the car you notice them everywhere.

If you find yourself unable to notice much negative inner talk, be patient. It may be that you are so used to your inner critic that you might not even notice it. Notice any reoccurring themes that you may accept as true beliefs such as :

- I'm not good enough, not smart enough, not young enough, not old enough.
- I'm too stupid, too old, too fat, too ...
- What sort of things do you tell yourself you cannot do, or are not good at? e.g., handling money, programming the VCR, being on time.
- What goal have you been unable to accomplish, and what have you told yourself about it?
- What dreams have you given up on because you told yourself that they were unrealistic?

How many friends would you have if you told your friends the kind of things you tell yourself? How many of your friends would you keep if they told you the nasty negative things you tell yourself? Why do we do this, how can we change it, and how will our lives become different when we do? What you are now and what you will become and accomplish is totally based on your beliefs (programs) about what you believe is possible for you.

Since your brain controls your behavior, it is imperative that it gets the right messages (programs) in order to get successful results. Given this knowledge, why would anyone not choose positive inner talk and success? Every situation can be approached this way. Turning your inner critic into your Inner Coach will be your most powerful tool for success.

Imagine having a huge advantage before you tackle any problem. Using positive inner talk first is the key to achieving your goals. What you say to yourself determines your beliefs; your beliefs determine your attitudes; your attitudes create your feelings about any situation; your feelings determine what action you will or will not take; and your actions, obviously, determine your results.

Isn't it time to take a close look at what has been limiting you? Why would anyone not choose positive inner talk and success vs. negative limiting talk? Since the old programming has not been working for you, GET RID OF IT, and REPLACE it with programming that works for you. We need to give ourselves explicit instructions for what we DO want.

Activity #2 "Thinking Big" board

Every choice you have made of what to think and what to do has brought you to where you are now. Even no decision is a decision resulting in loss of time and opportunities. Making powerful choices without listening to your inner critic will help you get the extraordinary life you want. In order to make the right choices for yourself you have to know what you want and where you want to end up; have a goal.

1. Choose a color poster board that energizes you. (Don't let your critic choose a safe color.)

2. Tune into your intuition and start collecting things that draw you to them, that speak to you, cut out pictures in magazines, draw, write, take pictures, and mount them on your board. Play! Don't limit yourself based on the past - only limit yourself to the dreams and things that you really love. If you want a red car, make sure it's red on your board.

3. Discover what you want your extraordinary life to look like in every area: House -geographical area, design, color, organization; Family/Friends - time spent with, activities, children; Career - balance with home life, type of work, income you desire, hours you work, location; Recreation; Spirituality; contribution to the world. If you need help determining your wants and needs, work with a coach to help you clarify what you want your extraordinary life to look like.

Now that you have created your "Thinking Big" board you can use your Inner Coach to reach these goals. It is time to play big!

Winners from every walk of life know and use the power of positive Inner Talk. Professional athletes all have coaches that help them improve their skills and inspire them to great feats, but it is the inner talk that is what counts when in the game. Can you imagine Tiger Woods saying to himself, "I'll never make this putt"? No, he is focused on thoughts of the ball going exactly where he wants it to go. Arnold Schwarzenegger envisioned himself and spoke of being the #1 movie star in the United States, when in reality his accent was too thick, and his first movie was a box office flop. Powerful, positive, present tense inner talk is what makes successful people successful. It is the driving force behind every action and decision. They see solutions and challenges instead of problems. You, too, have the ability to use this same tool; you have to think you can before you can.

When changing your negative inner talk to positive inner talk, there are several guidelines to follow:

- It needs to be in the present tense, as if it is already accomplished. If you state your positive talk in the future, your subconscious will keep it there in the future. Hence the joke about doing something tomorrow because tomorrow never comes. For example:"I make $10,000 per month."
- State the desired results in powerful language. Use lots of adjectives when describing your vision of what you want.When you say it, it should evoke the emotion of having achieved the goal. For example:"I enjoy being in fantastic shape. My body feels powerful, strong, and capable of doing anything. My mind is sharp and clear from invigorating exercise."
- The positive self talk that you create needs to be repeated frequently to overcome the programming of years of negativity.
- Create positive inner talk for each angle of the challenge you are facing. For example, for a job interview, picture each step of the process. "I look great, and my clothes are flattering and make me look my best. I make a great first impression. I am relaxed and confidently answer all the interviewer's questions. I present myself intelligently as the best candidate for the position that I want.I come across as a great person for the job."
- Don't worry if this sounds like you are lying to yourself. Your subconscious mind cannot determine if the information you are giving it is true - it just accepts it as true and works to create the desired results.

Give your subconscious directions for what you WANT as desired actions and results, and your subconscious will work to produce those results. Try some simple experiments with this, and you will be amazed by the results. You will wonder why everyone isn't using these secrets for success.

Activity #3 Reframe your negative beliefs into positive inner talk

Take out your notebook and look at the negative beliefs about yourself that you have listed there. In order to reprogram your subconscious, it is important to start sending it the messages that you want to see result in physical accomplishments in your life. Examine those negative beliefs that you are telling yourself and restate them in the positive. For example:

> "I am too old." Change to: "My wisdom and experience help me achieve all of my goals".

> "I always fail." Change to: "I believe in myself, I achieve the goals that I set with ease and joy in each step."

> "I can't do it." Change to: "I know that all things are possible and I am capable of achieving any goal I set."

Now that you are aware of your negative thoughts you can consciously stop the thought and replace it with a positive message to send to your subconscious. Practice repeating the positive statements you have created, post them where you will see them on your bathroom mirror, or in your day planner. Create tapes of your positive inner talk to listen to when you are getting ready for your day, or driving, so when you hear your inner critic start talking, you know what to say to him.

It is important to reframe your negative beliefs about yourself so that you have a strong foundation when you use Inner Coaching to achieve any goal you have. Take a look at how this works for weight loss, compared to how millions of desperate people approach weight loss. They see an ad that promises them the results they want. The ad provides external motivation. This motivation can work for a while in ideal situations, but what happens is that this external motivation does not cover all angles of the problem. What happens when:

- You have so much weight to lose that you become discouraged?
- You travel on business or vacation?
- You eat out a lot?
- The holidays arrive?
- You are depressed, angry, or sad?
- You hate to exercise?
- You can't afford to buy equipment or join a gym?

The solution with Inner Coaching is that you have formulated what you want and need to have happen before it does happen. It prepares you to face each situation in a way that moves you closer to your goal instead of letting the situations give you an excuse for failure. IT works!

Every goal you have that you either reach or fail to reach, regardless of how big or how small, essentially follows the same process:

1. You set your goal.
2. You determine the action steps you will need to take to reach it.
3. You set your intentions and commit to taking the necessary steps.
4. Your Inner Talk either talks you into or out of taking each step towards your desired outcome.
5. You either take or do not take the appropriate action.
6. Your Inner Talk will again determine what you do or do not do to continue toward your goal.

Obviously, what you are saying to yourself has a huge impact on whether or not you succeed at reaching your goal. So it is important to create positive self talk for each step you need to take to reach your goal, so when you start to talk yourself out of moving in the direction of your desired outcome, you are prepared to talk yourself into taking the necessary action.

Let's say your goal is to lose 12 pounds and to increase your fitness level in the next 90 days. Some of the action steps you determine you need to take in order to accomplish the goal are:

1. Eat smaller portions
2. Eliminate sweets
3. Eat more fruits and vegetables
4. Reduce intake of fats and carbohydrates
5. Do aerobic exercise for 40 minutes 3 times per week
6. Do weight training exercise for 40 minutes 3 times per week
7. Drink more water

The intentions you set are as follows:

1. Begin on the first of next month
2. Get rid of foods that are off limits
3. Stock up on healthy choice foods
4. Get up 1 hour earlier, daily, to exercise

Everything seems like this plan "should" work - if only you can maintain your willpower. The problem with this plan is that it is not a lack of willpower that will pull you off track and keep you from reaching your goal. IT IS YOUR OWN NEGATIVE INNER TALK THAT IS GOING TO UNDERMINE YOUR EFFORTS AND CREATE FAILURE IN REACHING YOUR GOAL.

What happens is something like this. The first turns out to be the day of a big party you need and want to attend. Immediately, your Inner Gremlins start to tell you:

"OK, so today is not the ideal day to start the diet."

"One day won't matter; I will start tomorrow instead of today."

"I will feel embarrassed to have to explain to everyone why I am not eating/drinking like usual."

"I don't want people to know my plan since I have always failed before."

"Since I am not going to eat like this for 90 days, I might as well enjoy this last party," etc.

This same sort of scenario is usually repeated at some point with each intention you have set.

THE NEGATIVE SELF TALK ACTUALLY GIVES YOU PERMISSION AND AN EXCUSE TO FAIL WHENEVER YOU MEET AN OBSTACLE AND THE GOING GETS TOUGH.

When the alarm goes off one hour early you start saying things like:

"Today is going to be such a busy day at work, I shouldn't tire myself before it starts."

"I didn't sleep well, so I need to try to sleep more than I need to exercise today."

"I am too sore from yesterday."

"My allergies, headache, whatever, are too bad," etc.

The secret to eliminating the negative self talk that has won over your good intentions in the past, is to consciously (at first) create a positive self talk for each scenario that you may encounter. When the negative self talk says it won't matter if you start on your goal one day later than planned, the positive self talk says:

"I am proud of myself when I stick to the plan that is best for me."

"I always make healthy choices."

"I am always in control of what I choose to eat."

When the alarm goes off and your negative self tries to talk you into rolling over for an extra hour of sleep, tune into your Inner Coach and ask yourself a question: "If I do what that inner voice says, will it take me closer to my goal or farther from my goal?" Then use the positive self talk that you have created to get yourself out of bed.

> "I get great satisfaction from doing what I set out to do."

> "Exercise makes me look and feel my best."

> "I love the results I get from healthy choices."

> "Having a trim and fit body makes me feel good about myself."

Once you get the gist of this process, it becomes easy to think of 12 or more positive statements regarding each choice you are making. (The more you can come up with, the stronger your convictions will become.)

When each situation arises that the gremlins are giving you an excuse for, use your Inner Coach and ask some questions: "What is the result that I want, and how can I change this excuse into a positive statement that will help me achieve that result?"

It is important to cover every angle and situation surrounding your goal. For example, in the case of diet and fitness as a goal, you will probably need to have positive self talk set up for:

1. Procrastination
2. Food choices
3. Serving sizes
4. Eating out
5. Holiday/special occasions/vacations
6. Eating on the run
7. Snacks
8. Hitting a plateau
9. Discouragement

Exercise:

1. Procrastination
2. Weather - if exercising outdoors
3. Travel
4. Tiredness
5. Boredom
6. Soreness
7. Lack of equipment or money for joining a health club
8. Not enough time
9. Feeling it is too difficult

Activity #4 Turn your goals into reality

1. You can use this Inner Coaching to improve every area of your life. Take each goal you have on your Think Big board and take it through all the steps of the goal process.
2. Create positive inner talk to support you with each action step of your goal.
3. Use your Inner Coaching to talk you through when your gremlins start to act up.

Like the Boy Scouts, being prepared really pays big dividends. It really won't be long before this new positive self talk becomes natural. Then, LOOK OUT WORLD, HERE YOU COME! The results you get from this are truly amazing! You become your own success coach - available immediately 24/7 to help you meet any challenge you are facing.

You CAN and do choose what you allow yourself to say to yourself. What you say to yourself has and will continue to determine your life!

Try an experiment right now with this process. Turn off the TV and the negative talk, and talk yourself into doing something RIGHT NOW that you need or want to accomplish.

About Hylen Success Coaching

Our vision is to help facilitate people to think expansively and envision their success as a true possibility, within their grasp. We then partner with them to help make it a reality.

One of the tools we use to help people in their personal growth is Inner Talk. By working with clients to change negative, limiting, internal chatter and develop new, supportive inner talk statements, we assist the client in reinforcing their positive outcomes and help them achieve their goals.

Stacey Hylen was a top sales producer for a major corporation at the age of twenty-four. As a personal and business success coach, she has helped her clients achieve phenomenal growth. One client, as a result of working with Stacey, grew her retail business four hundred percent in two years.

Stacey is a professionally trained coach, having studied at Coach University, and is a member of The Philadelphia Area Coaches Alliance (PACA) and the International Coach Federation (ICF). She is a member of the Research and Development Team for Coachville.com, the premier online resource for the personal and business coaching industry.

Valerie Hylen has been the owner of several successful businesses, was a co-host of an ongoing television segment presenting successful parenting tips, and is the co-author of a non-fiction children's book.

Valerie has been trained at Comprehensive Coaching University (CCU) and has facilitated team building workshops with CCU founder, Terri Levine. She is a member of the Philadelphia Area Coaches Alliance (PACA) and the International Coach Federation. She is also on the Research and Development Team for Coachville.com.

Services provided by Hylen Success Coaching
- Personal and business success coaching.
- Seminars and workshops.
- Mastermind group facilitators.

Hylen Success Coaching
2014 Greens Way Circle
Collegeville, PA 19426
(610) 454-1196
www.HylenSuccessCoaching.com
Stacey@HylenSuccessCoaching.com
Valerie@HylenSuccessCoaching.com

11

Spirit Coaching: Transforming Ourselves, Organizations and the World!

by Sharon C. Wilson, Dory Willer & Carolyn Wilson-Elliott

*E*ach of us approached the writing of this chapter from very different perspectives and backgrounds. Sharon Wilson, a former Corporate Executive, is co-founder of Coaching From Spirit, an evolving community of transformational coaches that brings Spirit out of the closet and into the coaching journey for practical results. Dory Willer, a Human Resources Executive, is the driving force behind Beacon Quest Coaching, providing career and life renewal coaching services for groups, couples, individuals, and organizations. Carolyn Wilson-Elliott, a published author specializing in vision and spiritual development, is one of the co-founders of Quantum Spirit International, helping organizations and people, including children and adults with disabilities, manifest their vision of a Purposeful Life.

As executives and managers, we rely upon our intelligence to manage groups effectively. Most of us think of intelligence as our individual capacity to learn, solve problems, and make sense of the world. But there are more dimensions to intelligence than just brains and logic. Our bodies, minds, hearts, and spirits also contain a wide spectrum of intelligences. When we integrate all of these different kinds of intelligence—emotional, analytical, intuitive, kinesthetic, narrative, and moral—we shift from trying to predict and control our world, to creatively responding to the world, and eventually, to flowing with the world.

Corporations and not-for-profit organizations are living systems that reflect the flow of their members' deeper intelligence. Members of a group exhibiting signs of stress, burn out, and/or loss of productivity, reflect an organization's inability to tap into and learn from the deeper intelligence of its members. There are no "right" or "wrong" ways to learn deeper intelligence; it only requires identifying, learning, and practicing new skills.

As Spirit Coaches, we know you are constantly receiving information from your deeper intelligence and that this information is your Inner Guidance. We believe that Spirit is coaching you through your deeper intelligence, and our job is to hold open an energy channel or pathway that assists you into more powerful shifts, transformations, and re-patterning as directed by your INNER COACH for the highest good of all concerned.

Co-creating a new way of life or a new way of managing a company requires the skills and abilities to tap into our inner guidance. It is different from co-operation, where everyone comes together for a specific goal—building a church, raising money for a charity, starting a business—and is expected to put the goals and visions of the group ahead of their individual needs and desires.

Co-creation begins with people knowing consciously that out of the act of being together, the co-creation of goals and visions will arise. That's what happened when Sharon was approached to write this chapter. She was already consciously joined to Dory and Carolyn. She liked being with them, and they had already created some powerful visions together. Sharon recognized that co-creating this chapter with other successful and effective Spirit Coaches would offer the most comprehensive perspective on this emerging professional niche of coaching and show the benefits that an individual or organization can achieve by working with this transformational coaching model.

We'd like to share with you how this chapter was co-created to illustrate the skills needed for a Spirit-led collaboration, some of the tools we used to move through blocks and obstacles, and how we energetically supported one another, not only in writing the chapter, but in the personal aspects of our lives that impacted our working together.

Although we have diverse experiences and visions, all three of us subscribe to the belief that everything happening in our lives—even those things that seem negative or fearful or even just irritating—is mirroring back to us our relationship with our inner Self. We also believe that Spirit is coaching us in every moment; that we have an opportunity with each experience to develop the skills needed to recognize the guidance we're receiving.

As you read the story of this chapter's birth, you'll see examples of Spirit at work in our lives and work experiences. And you will have an opportunity to allow Spirit to coach you! You will be experiencing our situations and see the mirror in it for you. You'll feel the questions we asked ourselves that allowed us to hear Spirit's messages. You can experience Spirit coaching by asking yourself the same questions. And if you choose to enter this place of experiencing and questioning, you will understand more about Spirit coaching— a process that we have no real logical explanation for, but is a process that brings forth a feeling of hope for us as individuals, as corporations, as a society, and as a world.

Take whatever resonates for you in this chapter and leave the rest. Allow the chapter to wash over you, and ask your inner guidance what wants to be born in you, in your company, and in your life. Then notice what shows up. Notice your dreams, your chance meetings, your conversations, and your feelings. Spirit will be coaching you, and as you are ready to accept the messages, you will begin to see them EVERYWHERE. Look for them in the mundane and the ordinary. The messages are coming through to you all the time.

Getting connected to Spirit

So, how did the CEOs of three separate organizations come together, allow Spirit to guide them in writing this chapter, and leave their egos at the door? We began with the intentions we were holding for this chapter. We got together and began defining our intentions and put them in writing:

> *We now state our intention to partner with Spirit and one another and ask for the highest guidance on the words to write for this chapter. We open to Spirit and allow the highest energy possible to surge through us. Our intention is to serve in the highest way those who are calling this work to them. Let us touch their hearts and activate their KNOWINGNESS to their grandest possibilities. We see it done and we give thanks! AMEN*

While we didn't have a clue about how we were going to do this, consciously defining our intentions set our energy in motion and began attracting situations and experiences we needed to co-create this chapter. Almost immediately, we were contacted by a cutting edge publication looking for information about the spiritual aspects of coaching. We invoked Spirit to help identify the questions and answers that would help a person know when they could benefit from Spirit Coaching. We joyfully embraced this opportunity, knowing it would help us get focused about writing the chapter for this book.

The next situation that appeared was seemingly an obstacle. Sharon was having difficulty focusing in on our scheduled meetings about the chapter. We were not making any progress, but we didn't focus on what was NOT happening. We did not blame Sharon for her inadequate performance. We chose, as Spirit coaches, to look behind our colleague's inability to perform according to our expectations, to see what was in

Sharon's inner landscape of thoughts and feelings that was creating this procrastination. There was something that needed to be addressed in her for her creativity and focus to return. We recognized this was an opportunity for Spirit to coach us all. It's also an opportunity for you to be coached by Spirit. As you read Sharon's story, notice the reactions you're having in your body. What emotions are showing up?

I was dealing with the emotional loss of a coaching colleague who had played an instrumental part in evolving Coaching From Spirit. Our relationship had meant a lot to me, and several months ago, she'd left to pursue some projects that called to her. I was in emotional shock as I realized that not only would she not be a part of the organization at this time, and possibly not ever, but our friendship, once filled with frequent deep conversations and sharing, was nearly non-existent.

I literally went into a period of mourning; the perceived loss of this individual was agonizing, and I wished I could do something to "get her back." I began beating myself up for experiences we'd had, thinking if only I would have been more, done more for her, she would still be with me. All my old patterns of rejection and feelings of abandonment surfaced, and while I tried to deny these emotions and push them away, they bubbled to the surface, and each day I felt sadder and sadder, wondering how I could fix it all.

As I began to write this chapter, I was guided to ask for a Spirit coaching session for myself from one of my collaborators. This led to a series of sessions each progressively more impacting and life changing than the previous one. I called her because the pain of feeling rejected by this person had become so great that I was feeling a deep heaviness in my chest area. I knew it was blocking me from focusing my energy on projects like this chapter. I knew I needed to deal with this situation and to be willing to explore what was causing me so much pain. I had been blaming my former colleague for just dropping out of sight, never calling me, and in general, simply eliminating me from her life. The pain of that was almost too much to bear.

I began by telling my collaborator what I was feeling. I told her I felt sad, rejected, and while I knew it was illogical - I felt unloved. She asked me to breathe into the feeling of rejection and to tell her where it was showing up in my body. I felt it in my heart and my stomach. She asked me to breathe into the feelings and let the feelings talk to me, to imagine what the feeling looked like, and what it wanted to tell me.

Throughout our whole session, images of times I felt rejected or betrayed, and therefore unloved, kept surfacing, and I kept breathing into them and asking questions. During the session, a part of me that felt I was emotionally responsible for this colleague surfaced, and I was able to give myself permission to see that I was not responsible for others.

I saw in that session that I'd experienced many situations in the past where I had set myself up to be an emotional rescuer for others. By doing that I had not taken care of "me" and I was angry with myself for that. In this session, I embraced all of my feelings and past actions and forgave myself. A great weight was lifted from me. By the end of the session, I felt no heaviness in my heart.

I needed to experience fully this new way of BEING! Now I was on fire to see what more wanted to be born in me! At that moment I could say, "I would not have changed a thing." I was free!

Getting out of Spirit's way

Allowing a colleague's personal crisis to enter our collaborative efforts was contrary to how we learned to function in the corporate world. In the past, we would have expected Sharon to ignore her feelings and get on with the job at hand. Most of us were never given models and processes for blending the elements of science, spirituality, personal growth, and coaching into a cohesive process that can be used to make more effective choices. Human beings raised us who had their own fears and judgments, which were then passed on to us. We then bring all these inherited fears and judgments into our relationships and to the workplace, without any sense of safety to honor our wounds and see them as opportunities for spiritual and organizational growth.

In our work as Spirit Coaches, we work with individuals and groups to help them better understand this blended process, as we have come to know it. We see it working effectively in our lives and our clients' lives. We help activate this blending of principles in a practical way to get results. So, following our own practices, we tapped into Sharon's experience to provide us with an energetic blueprint to begin the positive ripple effect that would transform ourselves, the chapter, and somewhere down the road, everyone who reads this.

We began by asking ourselves the questions we ask our clients:

> What kind of physical and/or emotional reaction did we have to Sharon's experience?
>
> How is that reaction guidance from Spirit?
>
> What is showing up in our lives that is similar to Sharon's experience?
>
> What theme or pattern of relating to others is showing up?
>
> What wants to be born from this theme? What do we desire in our lives?
>
> What do we want more guidance around?

As the three of us processed our experiences—Sharon's sharing of her experience while Dory and Carolyn experienced the receiving of that sharing—we received guidance around the form this chapter would take: invite the reader to experience our story and get a taste of Spirit Coaching by guiding them through their own responses.

Our energy surged at this prospect. Our enthusiasm for the chapter reached an all-time high, and we went off to work on our respective sections. A week later, we came together to find a new obstacle in our path. Dory was experiencing doubts about her value in this collaboration.

> *My enthusiasm was high, my confidence was solid, and I did what I knew how to do best. I tapped in, tuned in, and turned on my Inner Coach to filter out the stuff in my head and to speak from my heart. Voila, I produced a heartfelt explanation about Spirit Coaching. The only thing that was left for me to do was choose from the many stories of clients and their successes, and my portion of the chapter would be complete.*
>
> *Something changed though… a discussion about the examples and the stories needing to be "about us". Well, that's when I ended up with a major clog in my pipe; this was moving to a deeper well and requiring more disclosure about myself at a personal level.*
>
> *I reached a point that I just couldn't write or produce the remainder of the story. Thoughts would pop into my mind such as "Who would care what you went through?" "What makes you think your story would be of interest?" "Who do you think would relate to you?" And procrastination set in. I could not even think of the project without another limiting thought coming to mind immediately.*
>
> *As I shared my stuck position with Sharon and Carolyn, they quickly went into action, employing the coaching tools we had all learned to live and love by.*

It took more than just one or two chats to help move these boulders, and in reality, those coaching triad sessions led me back to what I knew all along. To use the tools on myself: that I had the best Inner Coach, which was within me. The answers and all that which was perfect for this chapter would indeed come forth, if I would allow it.

And so I asked my Inner Coach to assist and bring me to a place of feeling more positive about myself, and more secure with this project. The request was all that was needed, for then, as I've learned before, just stepping aside and watching for the bread crumbs placed in front of me — those synchronistic conversations, thoughts that pop in out of the blue, and the guidance that comes in the ordinariness of life when we pay attention to it - is all that is ever necessary. My work is to pick up the bread crumbs and follow the inspired path to action. That thought process (a coaching tool) would lead me to inspired thoughts, ideas, and action that would produce easy and effortless results, without the sweat.

Getting what we want

Dory's experience reminded us that Divine Guidance often comes in the guise of ordinary life. Writing part of this chapter gave her the impetus to "come out of the closet," to risk letting the world see her as a Spirit Coach, but Spirit wasn't going to let her stop there. She was going to have to do more than change her professional label. She was going to have to show the world what living with Spirit meant—revealing her vulnerability.

We receive guidance from Spirit in the form of emotions. In Spirit Coaching, all emotions fall into one of two categories: Love or Fear. Love-based responses show up in our bodies as a sense of expansiveness, relaxation, and/or increased energy. When our body is responding with Love, we feel safe to be who we really are, and we are drawn/attracted to the situation/person that makes us feel this way.

133

Fear-based reactions inhibit us and make our body feel constricted, anxious and/or drained of energy. When our body is reacting to Fear, we tend to avoid, confront, and/or judge the situation/person as negative.

When Dory's fears surfaced, she initially had difficulty staying with the fearful emotions in order to find the false thoughts she was telling herself. Those thoughts/beliefs were causing the writing block and questioning her worthiness in the collaboration. But her intention was to connect to the Guidance being offered, so she took action and asked Sharon and Carolyn to help her stay in that place of fear so she could receive the guidance. With the loving support of two people who honored her courage to face her fears, Dory began the questioning process:

- How is my body feeling? Constricted or expansive?
- Am I feeling love or fear? (As soon as she could say "I'm afraid," she felt the fear ease up, begin to dissipate; moving into a place of Observer, a more detached place.)
- Where is the emotion being held in my body?
- How is Spirit coaching me now?

At no time during the triad coaching sessions did Sharon or Carolyn give Dory answers or solutions to her experience. They guided her through the process, but they let Dory find the significance of the messages she was receiving. They asked her gentle questions to clarify what she was feeling and what she wanted to experience, and together, they held the vision in their consciousness of Dory at peace and in the condition she wanted to be in, which was feeling happy and having a deep sense of her value in this project. They saw her allowing Spirit to coach her and to allow in the guidance. By holding this vision for Dory and holding the strong belief for her that this was possible, they helped her activate that true knowing in her.

Spirit Coaching is a Spiritual Partnering of two or more equals coming together for the purpose of spiritual growth.

How we see ourselves right now, in this moment, is a reflection of how others have seen us all of our lives. If we're not happy about how we see ourselves, we need new mirrors to reflect our Authentic Nature. The most empowering thing we can do for ourselves is to Honor our Self enough to find those new mirrors.

Most of us already have plenty of negative energy sponsors in our lives—those who tell us "it can't be done," or those who drain us. At first, we may have to pay someone to be our new mirror—a coach, therapist, counselor, personal trainer—until we develop the skills to attract other positive energy sponsors into all areas of our life. Honoring our Self enough to invest in learning these skills will be the most challenging thing we ever do. But it will also be the most rewarding. Because once learned, we become our own Positive Energy Sponsor and begin to live the life we know, deep down, we're meant to live.

When we take the concept of Spiritual Partnering to the next level, we begin to see our interactions with every person and situation in our lives as an opportunity for spiritual healing and growth. Everyone, even the person we pass on the street, becomes a Spiritual Partner; a crucial part of our spiritual journey. It no longer matters if the other person consciously holds the intention to partner with us. It only matters that we hold the intention.

Even before the opportunity to work together on this chapter, Carolyn had been consciously holding the intention to manifest peace and harmony in the relationship between her son and herself, and her ex-husband and herself. In fact, she had been working on this intention for several years, and each interaction became a little more harmonious and peaceful than the one before.

In the fourth week of our collaboration, Carolyn took advantage of an opportunity to have her intentions for peace and harmony amplified and strengthened by participating in a group energy session with eight other Spirit Coaches. Within three days, the energy of the amplified intentions was having an impact on her life—but it didn't look anything like peace and harmony. Almost overnight, the situation with her ex-husband threatened to become litigious. Carolyn felt overwhelmed and threatened at a core survival level.

Carolyn became angry with her ex-husband, blaming him for the situation. For days, she held her anger as a protective shield against the primal fears that were surfacing. The anger interfered with her abilities to function effectively as a parent, a coach, a CEO. Finally, after several days of missing deadlines and appointments, Carolyn called a fellow Spirit Coach and asked for help. Her colleague led her through a visualization in which Carolyn saw all of her issues with her ex as rocks, stones, and pebbles loaded into a backpack.

> *She directs me to a small footbridge spanning a river of healing, loving waters. I stop halfway across the bridge and open the backpack. I pull out the first rock. It is an old friend, abandonment. I hold it, touching the rough surface, feeling the emptiness of the emotion in my body. When I am ready, I toss it into the river and watch, transfixed by the changing colors as the rock is transformed by the loving energy.*

> *I continue emptying the backpack, revisiting old, familiar issues I've been working on for years: self-worth, loneliness, betrayal. At the bottom of the pack is an unfamiliar issue. A small pebble, the size of a marble, dense and heavy. I hold it in my hands, waiting for guidance.*

> *Sobs burst forth from my heart chakra. It is guilt. A very old guilt. Time swirls around me, the past and future blending into the present. I am two years old, maybe three. My father is ill. He is changed. He is in pain. The guilt is born in that moment: guilt that I cannot alleviate his pain. I cannot make him laugh.*

> *Every moment of my life takes on a new meaning. The buried guilt motivating my every action: if I don't fix the pain, I am not worthy.*

This is my story. This is what I've been telling myself since the birth of that guilt. Now that the story is out, I can begin to change it, re-script it, and find new evidence of my worthiness. The evidence is already there. I just haven't let it in yet because it didn't fit my story. Every compliment, thank you, or gift I've received over the years has been deflected, pushed away, because that little girl knew she wasn't any good. Now, I can re-visit those moments of acceptance in a new light, and begin to let the love and acceptance into my heart.

Is this how I expected peace and harmony to manifest in my life? Not at all. At some level, I was expecting my ex-husband's behavior to change too. But this inner peace and harmony is much more than I ever expected. I will love myself in a new way now that I have found a new level of self-acceptance. And I know it will affect my interactions with everyone else in my life. I will judge myself and others less harshly. I will love others in a new way.

Letting Spirit coach you

Carolyn's story is an example of Spirit coaching us through our everyday interactions and conflicts. Her son's pain triggered a reaction in her, reminding her of some pain she had disowned. Ignoring her pain brought about a period of seeming chaos as her ability to cope with the world continued to decline. She felt disconnected from Spirit, but in actuality, Spirit was sending her guidance in the form of chaos, which is really only contrast.

Contrast shows up in our life when we have a high degree of desire for something—in Carolyn's case, peace and harmony—and a high degree of resistance or belief that it's not possible—while Carolyn desired peace and harmony, her past experiences had proven to her that she was helpless to bring it about. While it looked like everything was falling apart in Carolyn's life, it was really beginning to fall together.

As long as Carolyn moved through her contrast unconsciously, she was living her life by default, unable to impact the situation except to increase the conflict. We give up our power when we blame other people or situations for what we are feeling. While Carolyn continued to judge her ex-husband, she was giving her power away to what was happening around her, leaving her powerless to change the situation or her feelings.

All three of us had a high desire to write this chapter and to assist others in awakening their Inner Coaches, but there was resistance—stories we were telling ourselves that blocked us from moving to the next level of our own personal power and excellence. These stories, or beliefs, are just thoughts we keep thinking again and again. They create feelings in us, and those feelings are the vibrations that attract our circumstances to us.

In each story, our beliefs and feelings attracted outside experiences that offered us an opportunity to identify not only the beliefs, but the parts of us that were holding those beliefs in place! By embracing those parts of us, we began to see the true guidance offered in these seemingly mundane, even irritating experiences: that it is always about us! When we reach this awareness, we can tap into the greatest sense of personal power. A personal power that creates personal excellence and lives of love, joy, peace, prosperity, and balance.

Everything that happens in our lives is an opportunity for greater clarity about what we truly want. When we judge a situation as "good" or "bad," we are actually giving our power away to what's happening to us. We mistakenly think we are powerless to affect what is showing up in our life and powerless to create the new experiences that we want. We see our life situations as evidence that supports our limiting beliefs around our sense of unworthiness. For example, we often hear clients and coaches telling us that their only desire is to be totally connected with Spirit. When we ask them what that would mean, they often reply, "If I am doing it right and am connected to Spirit all the time, no 'bad' things will happen to me and my life will be blissful." This judging of situations, individuals, and experiences as "good" or "bad" keeps the client in a place of powerlessness.

When we can reframe a situation—see things we do not want as "contrast"—then we can begin to ask the questions that help us see what is wanting to be born; what parts of ourselves need to be loved and embraced; and what old thoughts (beliefs) are causing our feelings that attract these situations. Only then do we view our life as a series of golden opportunities to allow our personal power and excellence to emerge.

We're all coaches. Whether we do it professionally or not. The skills are valuable in living an effective life. Next time you find yourself in a place of contrast—angry with another person, frustrated with yourself, procrastinating on a project, or simply feeling depressed or attacked by another—ask yourself if you're willing to shift to a place of peace or resolution. If you are willing, try the steps listed below. And remember, you can't do this wrong. There is no right or wrong way when we hold our intention to partner with Spirit.

Getting Connected to Spirit begins with your intention (willingness) to partner with Spirit in changing how you're feeling. Say a prayer that resonates for you. Affirm you are having an Inner Coach session and state your intentions to partner, and intentions for peace, in this experience. It may help to use a symbol or image of your Inner Coach. It can be anyone you admire and aspire to be like, such as a famous person, a fictional character, or a saint or Master like Jesus, Buddha, Mother Mary, Kuan Yin. Anyone who feels good for you will work.

Ask for help. It can be as simple as saying aloud or silently, "OK, Inner Coach, I'm ready to look at this in a new way. I want to feel peace. Coach me." Hold the intention to partner with your inner guidance. This engages your inner guide immediately.

Getting out of Spirit's Way means opening to the possibility that the beliefs and emotions you are feeling are not set in concrete, that your reality doesn't have to be what you are currently experiencing.

Look for the underlying belief that is causing your feelings. Ask your Inner Coach to help you to tap into the story your body, emotions, and thoughts are telling you. What is the emotion you're feeling—pain, anger, victimization, resentment, depression? Where is that emotion showing up in your body? When have you felt this way at other times in the past? How has this been a theme in your life? Ask these questions and then wait for information to pop into your mind; a feeling, a thought, a memory. Just notice it—it is all guidance from your Inner Coach, even if it seems to make no real sense.

Ask your Inner Coach, "What am I afraid of in this situation?" After you get an initial thought then ask your Inner Coach to help you connect with the next level of fear or worry. Often it will be rooted in worry about possible future events, or regrets around past events/experiences. Keep asking your Inner Coach, "What lies under that?" Eventually, you'll come to the core beliefs you're holding.

Let go of the expectation that you'll find all the answers in one session. We're not biologically hardwired to experience Spirit or God in its totality. Instead, we get glimpses throughout our lives. Guidance may show up later in the day, or in a conversation, or another contrasting experience. In the examples we shared with you, we went through multiple sessions with one another and our own Inner Coaches to help us make baby shifts in our connection to Spirit. Be gentle with yourself.

Ask your Inner Coach, "Help me to be willing to let this go." You may want to see white light around you (or another) and simply let go of how this will all be resolved. We are all energetically interconnected, so doing this kind of energy work can make a profound impact on you and everyone in your life. In reality it is affecting every person on the planet. This intention for peace in relationship contrasts can deeply affect the other person without ever having a physical conversation about the issue.

Getting What You Want comes from the contrast you're currently experiencing: the contrast shows you what you want to be feeling. For example, if you're angry, you may want to feel charitable or loving or just detached. The unwanted emotion is coming from the beliefs you're holding. Ask your Inner Coach to help you remember some past situation in which you felt charitable or loving or detached. What was the belief you were holding at that time? Feel the emotion that is the result of that belief.

Begin to see that the current situation is about you, about the belief you are holding. Ask your Inner Coach for assistance to shift. You don't need to do this alone. And then, wait for the inspiration, the ideas, and the actions that come up. The first thing that comes up, don't judge it. Feel it. If the idea or action brings you into feeling what you want to feel—charitable, loving, or detached—then that is True Guidance.

As you get clearer on your intentions and focus on seeing the guidance of each experience, synchronicities will occur, opportunities will flow to you, and miracles will become a part of your reality on a daily basis. You will begin to see how partnering with Spirit is the most logical thing to do in a world that seems so illogical at times. You will feel more peaceful, even in the midst of painful and contrasting experiences. And you will find yourself achieving your personal excellence in every area of your life

We hold the intention that by reading this information and applying some of these concepts and tools, you will begin to open the door to partner with Spirit in your life, work, and in each moment. Take a moment to ask what the value has been for you, not only in this chapter, but also in this book. There is a message here for you. You have picked up and read this book for a reason. What parts resonate with you? What guidance are you being given? What action wants to be taken?

We're honored to have had this opportunity to share our

stories with you. We deliberately moved into places of contrast, embraced our vulnerabilities, and opened our hearts, because we so strongly believe you can unlock your personal and professional excellence by partnering with Spirit for guidance.

About Sharon C. Wilson

Sharon C. Wilson is a Certified Spiritual Counselor, Founder and Chief Spiritual Officer of Coaching From Spirit. Coaching from Spirit is more than a spiritual coach training program, it is an evolving community of transformational coaches that bring Spirit out of the closet and into the coaching journey for practical results. She has coached hundreds of individuals and coaches in a proven process that provides a foundation for them to partner and trust their 'inner coach' to release old beliefs, patterns, and programs that can block them from allowing the reality they want. This process is effective for individuals and organizations. It creates a framework to intentionally align focused energy of thoughts, feelings, and actions to attract more of what they want. Sharon creates and guides transformational business programs in marketing and income building that blend science, spirituality, and personal success principles in an integrative and practical way. "I help the individuals, coaches, and companies I support to create new positive realities beyond what they think is 'realistic' and 'possible' by partnering with their 'inner coach' in a process that fits anyone's belief system. I guide 'out of the box' visionaries to make a quantum leap in thinking, feeling, and actions that creates more peace, fulfillment, and prosperity in all areas of their lives." Her background includes executive positions in sales, marketing, human resources, and consulting. She lives near Pittsburgh, Pennsylvania with her husband Robert and daughter Joy.

admin@coachingfromspirit.com

www.coachingfromspirit.com

About Dory Willer

Dory Willer believes in designing lives that include purpose and passion! That is the drive behind Beacon Quest Coaching which provides career and life renewal coaching services for groups, organizations, and individuals

of all ages. Drawing on two decades of human resource executive experience, Dory is a passionate champion for your spirit, providing the structure and process of creative discovery in assisting clients with finding and clarifying "what's next." Her private practice offers retreats for executive teams/boards, adults, teenagers, and couples. Additionally, she offers corporate and conference workshops, and is available for speaking engagements.

Dory holds a BS degree in Organizational Behavior along with an HR certification from Stanford University. Her previous career includes working in a Fortune 100, and as a Vice President of Human Resources. Willer holds additional advanced coaching certifications with LifeGuides™, Coaching from Spirit, and Life on Purpose Institute. She is chapter president of the International Coaches Federation, a member of the Society of Human Resource Professionals, and the National Speakers Association.

www.beaconquest.com
Dory@BeaconQuest.com

About Carolyn Wilson-Elliott

Carolyn Wilson-Elliott, a published author specializing in vision and spiritual development, is the CEO and one of the co-founders of Quantum Spirit International (QSI), an organization helping people—including children and adults with disabilities—manifest their vision of a Purposeful Life. A Certified Spiritual Life Coach and teleclass leader, Carolyn is the director of QSI's Living Out Loud Program™, a twelve-week course that enhances and develops spiritual growth through intentional play, body and emotional awareness, and narrative intelligence.

Carolyn sees her purpose in life as a Storyteller. "Humans tap into the sacredness of life each time they share their stories with one another," explains Carolyn. "Our stories hold the essence of our Divine Purpose. They allow us to heal and nurture our Self and Others." In her personal life, coaching, and workshops, Carolyn helps men and women discover and shape their own Life Stories. "Understanding the stories we tell our self serves as a catalyst to activate our Inner Guidance so we can live a Purposeful Life," she explains. "When we own our Story, we recognize the unique gifts that we alone bring forth into the Universe."

Carolyn also shares her stories, and the stories of others, through articles about family, genealogy, adoption, vision development, and spirituality. She is managing editor of *QuantumSpirit,* a monthly electronic publication about spiritual connections to work, family, community, and Self. Along with Katherine Nurek and Donna Wendelburg, co-founders of Achievers Unlimited of Wisconsin, Inc., a non-profit organization devoted to vision development education, Carolyn has co-authored three books on vision development: *Vision Development 0-3: An Observe & Play Workbook*; *Vision Development 4-5: Kindergarten Readiness*; and *Vision Development in the Classroom.* They've also written a number of educational booklets, including *Vision Development and ADD/ADHD* and *Computer Abused Eyes.*

Carolyn's articles have appeared in publications such as *Reunions magazine, Fields of Vision, The Developmental Delay Registry, Roots & Wings.* Some of her articles are available on the web at IdeaMarketers.com, FabulouslyFemale.com, QuantumSpirit.com, FlufflyMoose.com, OmPlace.com and AlternativeParenting.com.

Quantum Spirit International is located in Milwaukee, WI. Our staff consists of psychotherapists, artists, vision therapists, educators, and writers who strive to apply the principles of spirit coaching in their fields of expertise. We help other professionals and organizations incorporate these principles into their current programs and curriculums. For more information:

(414) 278-8698
www.quantumspirit.com

12

Let Your Space Be Your Coach:

How Feng Shui Can Unlock Your Inner Essence and Unleash Personal Power

by Maggie Burgisser

Personal excellence. Extraordinary life. Charmed existence. Terms as broad as all the aspects of great accomplishment we can think of collectively, or as precise as our own ambitions. What images soar before us as we envision our own excellence? What barriers do we imagine withhold this excellence? How can we know where our greatest potentials lie, and what needs to be overcome or set aside to reach them?

There are many avenues to personal excellence. One discussed in this book is coaching. A great coach helps you gain clarity about where you are now and where you want to go, and then supports you as you move towards your vision. Normally we think of being coached by another person, but here we will look at *Feng Shui*, the ancient Chinese art of placement, and how it reveals where we are and how to look within our space to move forward in life.

Our space sits before us like an open book; ready to show us how we are really thinking and feeling. Where we sit today is a perfect reflection of our inner being. Our surroundings are the outer expression of our inner essence.

Knowing this can be a great awakening or an appalling realization! But before we rush to draw conclusions, we must realize that our surroundings are only a mirror, not a judge and jury. There is a saying that goes:

> "A mirror does not hold anything, is not self-conscious, reflects everything, and never fails to tell the truth."

The language of Feng Shui is based on several thousand years of astute observation, trial and error, intuition, and spiritual discipline. Is it valid? One could think of it as a massive series of double blind studies. Does it work? Even though banned in China during the current Communist regime, it has survived and spread through the centuries. It acquired the name Feng Shui in the 9th century by Chinese Master Yang Yun-Sang who worked with the Yang dynasty.

The name *Feng Shui*, which means literally *Wind-Water*, is a catch-all term to emphasize that the discipline of Feng Shui is devoted to helping mankind live in harmony with the forces of nature. Wind and water are two of the most powerful natural forces and have the potential to destroy or enhance our lives.

Every major culture has had some system of describing and defining the most harmonious way to co-exist with nature. Feng Shui was introduced to the West about 20 years ago, mostly through the efforts of H. H. Professor Thomas Lin-Yun, Grandmaster of Tibetan Tantric Black Hat Feng Shui. As the West adapts to the principles of conscious use of space, the experience of other cultures is being included, thanks to the efforts of practitioners such as Denise Linn, with her native American background, or Karen Kingston and her study of Bali, as well as many others. Both of these world renowned authors and lecturers have studied Feng Shui principles in multiple cultures.

When we decipher the language of space, we have the opportunity to gain clarity about ourselves through the landscape we have created in our surroundings: how it supports us, protects us, nourishes us, and/or possibly holds us back.

We create our space in two ways. We create *physical surroundings*, and we create the subtler, but equally as vital, *interpretation* of our space.

We draw towards us surroundings known through our five physical senses. What we see, hear, touch, smell, and taste is energy in form. Through choices, some conscious, some unconscious, we select physical surroundings. We are learning also that we can attract objects to ourselves with our thoughts. We may select a brick house with a blue chair inside for sitting. We may be thinking we would like a yellow lamp and suddenly a friend arrives with a yellow lamp for a gift. We have created our surroundings through action and thought. This physical environment comprises the *mundane* factor in Feng Shui. We will want to know how chi or life-force moves around and through mundane objects, and its effect on us.

The other level of creation is through our *perception* of our surroundings. We might call this the illusionary aspect. We create the feelings attached to our surroundings.

In the classic story of the blind men and the elephant, each man places his hands on an elephant and then describes the part he has touched. Each observation is true, but distorted by its limited perception. For example, suppose the man who touches the tail of the elephant meets a dog and just happens to touch its tail also. He may come to the conclusion that all mammals are long and thin, distinguished only by their texture. Perceptual thoughts have incredible power. They create a contextual field that draws more reality towards us to validate our perceptions. On his next encounter with a mammal, the blind man may ignore all parts not meeting his perception of a mammal until he finds the tail. His experience will create a belief. Some kind of "seeing" will be necessary to alter his belief. That new view can totally change his emotional reaction and physical interaction with the object. Where previously the man was content to stand beside the elephant touching the tail, should he suddenly have the sense of sight, contentment may turn to fear and he may back away. Or he may feel intense awe and love for this newly found creature and hug its trunk. These perceptions are personal choices based on the information he has received through his senses.

Going back to the previous example, the yellow lamp may make us feel happy every time we look at it because we love the friend who gave it to us, or it may make us feel guilty every time we look at it because the friend spent too much money for it. In either case, we are creating an emotional climate that is very much a part of the environment where the lamp sits.

Our bodies are receiving massive amounts of information through our senses, including our sixth sense, all the time. Have you ever had the "chills" for no obvious reason when you entered a room, or walked into a room and wanted nothing more than to settle in and chat or read? Have you ever found yourself caught up in an argument in a place that is agitated and chaotic or been overcome with a sense of peace in a holy place? These feelings are created from the information we receive through all six senses. But it is just information. What remains constant is our ability to choose how we interpret this information. This is called *free will*.

What we are going to do now is see how we can use all this knowledge to let our space communicate with us. In Feng Shui, we are concerned with chi (interchangeable with terms such as life-force, force of nature, energy, prana, etc.), its movement, and changing form. It is important to understand how chi moves. Visualizing water helps us to imagine this.

Water can move in a straight line. This is useful if you want to move water somewhere quickly, like out of a fire hose at the scene of a fire. It is also useful if you are a fireman back home using a shower to clean up; however, you would not want the same amount of pressure.

Water can be still. Perfect if you want to see yourself in its reflection, but what if it is sitting in a bucket you forgot behind the tool shed in October, and it is now April? It may be more suitable for a scientist studying mosquito larvae.

Beauty Spa → Facial
massage ⟩ Wellness
Exercise Machines Steam
Small counter - for fresh juices, health food
café built after the estate war house.

Coaching → Bus. Administration
Marketing / Management Program

Seniors Counselling
Wellness — Metaphysical
Spa

Children - first University
- Success in their endeavour

pay all debts

Car
house

Water can move in a curving/spiraling/undulating motion. This would generally be considered harmonious, like a meandering river, but what if the river becomes shallow and exposes the underlying rocks? Fabulous if you are in a raft and have come out to ride the rapids, but not so wonderful if you are a swimmer and are unprepared and unprotected.

As you can see from these examples, it is all about *perspective* and *perception*. In each situation, the water moved in response to natural law. And each case had the potential to be appropriate or not, depending on the perspective of the person. Your opportunity as you observe nature manifest itself in your space is to see what it is telling you *about you*. Are you the Indian princess seeking her beauty in the reflecting pool, or the scientist looking for mosquito larvae? Are you the fireman at the scene of the fire, or the fireman back home needing to rejuvenate? Are you the white water enthusiast, or the surprised swimmer?

Constant in all this changing form and movement is nature's need to seek balance. Many of us are familiar with the Yin-Yang or Tai Chi symbol. The white spot in the black is the beginning of the change to white, and the black spot in the white is the beginning of the change to black.

Imagine how this symbol would look as a moving sphere. It is then a perfect symbol of nature seeking balance. Now imagine that every molecule of your body and your space is in the middle of this undulating sphere of chi. Are you fighting it, or going with the flow? What is keeping you centered or off center? How do you try to establish balance? How is natural law affecting your space as it tries to establish balance?

What appears out of balance may be like the top of the swing of a pendulum (or the tip of the Yin or Yang). As the pendulum returns, it reaches center, and for one moment it is in perfect balance. But what would happen if the pendulum somehow got stuck at the top of the upswing? Where would the compensation take place? Rest assured, nature will be seeking a way to balance the stuck pendulum. It could be that somewhere far out in the other direction a reaction will occur that seems totally unrelated.

Professional Feng Shui practitioners will always remind you that results cannot be predicted and things may appear worse before they are better. You can see from the pendulum example that it is a disclaimer with backup. Dire warnings you may hear in connection with Feng Shui observations stem from conclusions Feng Shui masters have drawn observing similar types of imbalances over a long period of time. These conclusions have crystallized into "rules". Are the predictions or rules absolute? Of course not. Are they probable? Yes, depending on how accurately the imbalance has been discerned.

What tools of Feng Shui have you gathered so far in this discussion? You have basic knowledge of the movement of chi as seen in the water example: straight line, static, or undulating. You have six senses to feel the chi. You have free will to interpret what you feel. You have the ability to be a mirror and suspend judgment of what you observe.

If you have been reading any books or heard some talks about Feng Shui you may be tempted to jump right in with the cures: crystals, wind chimes, water fountains, etc. But you wouldn't take medicine without a diagnosis, and so, this applies also in Feng Shui. Find out what you have created up to this point before you begin to recreate.

Let's take a look at your own space. Imagine yourself approaching your home or office. You are approaching the entrance. How does the traffic move towards it? Does it move quickly? Meander? Does it go directly towards your front door? Is the entrance hidden, requiring some moving around in order to be reached? Going back to the earlier water analogy, what can you learn about yourself as you answer these questions:

Moves quickly towards the entrance:
> Are you one who always feels under siege or overwhelmed?

Or

    Do you love having lots of activity; maybe you have a business in your home or lots of family and welcome the flow?

Meanders towards your entrance:

    Do you like coming home because it is so peaceful?

Or

    Do you feel it is pretty boring in your neighborhood because not much is happening?

Entrance is hidden:

    Nothing good comes your way and you often lose out on good opportunities?

Or

    You need to be fully protected from the outside world in order to rejuvenate and regain balance?

As you can see, it is not so much about what is happening in a given situation, as how it fits in with your particular needs.

Now ask yourself how you happened to come to live or work in this place? Did you consciously choose it for one of the above reasons? Do you feel like you ended up in the wrong place? Did someone else choose it? Did it happen accidentally, but now you have discovered an advantage to the situation? If you could change the situation, would you? Now that you have stepped back and taken a good look at the situation, do you have a new appreciation of it?

There is plenty of room for variety in interpretation. One person's nectar is another's poison. You owe it to yourself to create surroundings that nurture and support *you*. With time you can learn to interpret the signals of nature that allow you to know whether or not you are in a state of balance. Feng Shui cures come into play when a situation puts you *out* of balance.

In Black Hat Feng Shui, every situation is perfect. One is drawn to (or more accurately, draws onto oneself)

Move forward to escape from our suffering

circumstances that will create the opportunity for growth. If a circumstance seems to be creating hardship, it is, nonetheless, bringing into focus an aspect of yourself that is not in balance. An example of this could be a house at the end of a cul-de-sac. Traditionally, Feng Shui says that is a dangerous place to be. The straight line of chi is too forceful (like a fire hose) and with no outlet causes a lot of upheaval. Consequences could be divorce, bankruptcy, or other major upsets. But in truth, it may be that the occupants have a marriage or a financial situation that is already out of balance and this blast of chi is forcing the issue. The occupants may have been drawn there by a subconscious desire to bring balance to their lives and are not, as it might appear, just hapless victims of the whims of the universe.

For all of us, as our awareness, centeredness, and knowledge expands, we increase our ability to control the flow of life force using Feng Shui principles and interpret events in our lives using free will. *This is where personal power surges forward. We can recreate surroundings and control our perceptions.*

In the cul-de-sac example above, one could use methods to deflect and slow down the force of oncoming chi and use it more like a shower to clean up shaky finances, relationships, or whatever issue is coming into focus. As the cleansing is taking place, one's perception can be that it is causing suffering, *or* that it is creating freedom from past suffering. *It is in the interpretation of experience that we have absolute free will. And,* the energy we create around that circumstance through our interpretation of it has the power to draw to us *more of the same.*

There is a great analogy in Feng Shui about a snake in a pipe. Snakes can only move forward. Like this snake we must move forward to escape our suffering. When we are feeling the squeeze of the pipe we are not happy, but the trip is easier if we use any and all tools available to help, such as Feng Shui, *and* keep in mind that through this process we will reach our freedom from suffering.

Feng Shui practitioners notice that certain "life fortunes" (as seen on the Feng Shui map called the Bagua) come up frequently when people are seeking help. These are relationship (marriage), money, and health. In the West, we have the tendency to always want more of *all of the above.* But our true wishes may be hidden in our space.

It could be that a relationship corner is screaming, "I want to be left alone!", while the occupant is saying, "I want to get married!" This is why it is so important to get clarity in life before moving ahead. Perhaps, in this example, there is an intimacy issue left from past experience, and subconsciously the person knows it needs to be handled before he or she can move into a lasting relationship. To immediately add cures to the relationship corner may bring a new partner, but it will be doomed from the get-go. Far better to respond to the message your subconscious has created in your space, "Leave me alone, I'm not ready!" and build the personal foundation for partnership first.

Money is always a hot topic. Let's fix up that money corner, we all say with glee in our eyes. But the lesson may be that the way to have more is to better manage what we already have. We may need to look in the helpful people area (as seen on the bagua) or knowledge area and from there build true financial security.

Let's return to your space. Imagine yourself now sitting in your favorite room. What draws you there? Has it always been your favorite spot? Is it also the favorite room of other family members? Is it greatly different or similar to the favorite spot in your last residence? If you had a magic wand, what would you change? What would you leave the same? Does this room nurture and support all aspects of your life? Do you feel protected from adversity here? Are you top dog here, or are you accepting second (third, etc.) best? If it doesn't totally support you, are you willing to make the effort to create one spot that totally makes you happy?

As you move through these questions, what are you registering in your body? Words like warm, cool, full, empty, steady, falling, hollow, pulled in, pushed back, nauseated, can't breathe, lightheaded, grounded, heavy, open, balanced, imbalanced, etc., are some of the many valid physical reactions you may register in response to the chi of a space or place.

This is how your space coaches you. The answers to your questions and sensations in your body will tell you variations of the following conclusions:

> I'm scattered (life force moving too fast)
> I'm stuck (life force is static)
> I'm in the flow (life force is balanced)

Your mind, body, and spirit are constantly receiving and reacting to information from the environment. Conscious space design requires that you first interpret the messages of your space through the sensations in your body and the objective mirror of your mind. You can then recreate according to your choices.

Feng Shui is becoming popular. One of the things that is so fascinating about the USA is that it is truly a melting pot of cultures. The mixing of cultures has created losses such as separation from ethnic wisdom about use of space, and at the same time, brought the opportunity to refine that same wisdom as it is mixed with other cultures. We are, along with other modern Western cultures, creating our own special brand of conscious space design. There are many books now available on Feng Shui, each interpreting the discipline of conscious space design through the experiences of its author, and therefore, completely valid.

Remember, however, that your truths are unique and uniquely intertwined with your space(s). Your space is truly the outer image of your inner essence. Your space is there to assist and support you. Its secrets are discovered as much through asking the right questions as finding the right answers. *Unlock its wisdom and unleash your power.*

Create deep and lasting change in your life *today*. You don't need to move from your chair, lift the phone, or write a check. Just lift your eyes, open your senses, focus the mirror of your mind, and *see as you've never seen before!*

About Maggie Burgisser

Maggie Burgisser is President of Healthy Images, L.L.C., of Mount Laurel, New Jersey, USA. Passionate about the rewards of self-knowledge, Maggie has parlayed several disciplines into a comprehensive format that offers growth for individuals and businesses. As such, Healthy Images uses personal *coaching* to help individuals and business owners identify and pursue their most vital and driving goals. *Feng Shui* is used to create office or personal space totally supportive of their goals. To complete the link for businesses, *promotional tools*, including logos, brochures and effective advertising, are all designed to precisely reflect the goals and mission of the business. The results for clients have been to experience fast, deep change whether it is bringing into focus a course they are already on, or totally changing direction in their lives or businesses. Healthy Images' motto is *"Plant your feet and fly!"*

Ms. Burgisser has more than twenty years dental hygiene experience in the United States and Switzerland including private clinical practice, teaching, and public health. While living in England her career changed direction when she pursued a postgraduate degree in advertising administration. This followed her love for the *art of communication*, which has expanded into the realms of personal coaching and Feng Shui which is, of course, the art of communicating with one's surroundings. She became convinced of the effectiveness of Feng Shui when her husband's health was restored following their first Feng Shui consultation experience in their home/business.

Ms. Burgisser has a B.S. in Education/Dental Hygiene, Ohio State University, Postgraduate Diploma in Advertising Administration, Watford College, England, and has completed the Three Year Meditational Feng Shui Apprenticeship Program from Feng Shui Master Melani Lewandowski of Philadelphia, Pa. She has also studied with Feng Shui Grandmaster H.H. Prof. Thomas Lin Yun, as well as Karen Kingston and Lama Surya Das. She has completed Levels I and II training from Coaches Certification Institute

155

and is completing the Executive Coaches training program of Comprehensive Coaching U. She is a member of the American Dental Hygienists' Association, International Coach Federation, and is President of the Midatlantic Chapter of the International Feng Shui Guild.

Maggie lives in Mount Laurel, NJ, USA, in a constantly evolving, Feng Shui friendly home surrounded by an experimental co-creative garden. Living with all of this as gracefully as possible are her husband and two teenage children.

You may contact her at:

info@healthyimagesllc.com

Tel. (856) 802-1524

www.healthyimagesllc.com.

13
Intuition at
the Speed of Change

by Jeannine Ayres, Morgaine Beck, Suzee Ebeling,
Sharon Hooper, and Lauren Lee

"It is by intuition that we discover and by logic that we prove..."
HENRI POINCARE

In today's fast-paced world of the information super highway, electronics can reach us everywhere. We are bombarded with more information than ever before. Instead of making it easier for us to think and make decisions, information overload makes it harder. Wouldn't it be wonderful if you had secret powers to blast through this chaos and find the answer that works best for you? You do – it's called intuition and it moves at the speed of change.

"If you are going to succeed in chaos, you must connect with chaos; act in concert with it.
What does that mean?
It means that you must trust
in intuition, trust in self."
JIM TAYLOR AND WATTS WACKER

157

Maybe you recognize intuition as a hunch, an inner voice, gut instinct, common sense or inspiration. Whatever you name it, we invite you to listen to your intuition in a new way - to reawaken your natural instincts. You'll be honoring inherent wisdom, that silent place where you can tap into your inner knowledge.

There are many occasions in life when new, unanticipated situations call for immediate decisions. We often don't have the luxury of time to analyze and evaluate every possibility. Some of the challenges we face defy clear understanding - the meaning of illness, the ramifications of relationships, the concerns that keep us up at night. In each case, we are being called to 'let go' and take action based on a 'knowing' that lies beneath the conscious mind - intuition!

One way of letting go is to shift from using your logic to using your intuitive powers. A few years ago, one of our authors felt a sudden urge to visit her father who lived 70 miles away. Even though it appeared to be a totally impractical decision, she did it anyway. To her surprise, she arrived at her father's house at exactly the same time as her twin brother, with whom she had not spoken. They broke down the door and found their father lying on the floor, dying of a heart attack. Because they listened to their intuition, they were able to spend the last ten minutes of his life with him.

Sometimes you find yourself in a tight spot and you need a fast answer; try your intuition. A harried executive exclaimed that by the time he was ready to implement an innovative sales program in his 173 employee company, new information had flooded in to change the deductive reasoning that had led him to the original decisions.

"What do I do now?" he queried, close to desperation. "I'm in a real crisis! The board of directors wants an answer tomorrow. Do I scrap the original plan or implement a new one based on this new knowledge? Right now, I'm afraid to make the decision without more detailed research, but I know that my competitors will clobber us if we don't go forward immediately."

He felt paralyzed, unable to take a step without relying on his previous methods of data analysis and team advisories. His intuition coach suggested he turn the table upside down - literally. Sitting inside the conference table, he was able to see a new perspective and decided to implement an innovative new sales program that increased profitability by 15%. The executive solved his problem by integrating his intuition, knowledge, and experience.

Let's look at a real-life example of a coaching session where a client "S" and his coach "C" explore the client's intuition. To get the most out of the following dialogue, we recommend you take a moment to quiet your mind and then imagine you are the client. *What comments ring true for you? What do they remind you of? Where is this dynamic happening in your life today?*

Key moments in the dialogue are supported by "teachable moments" found on the opposite pages. The moments are: fear, synchronicity, Aha! moments, and symbols (the language of intuition).

Intuition Coaching in Action:
Transcript of an actual coaching dialogue;
A CASE STUDY.

S: How can I develop my intuition further, and how can I detect when it is speaking to me?

C: First, I'd like to ask if there was a time in your life when you felt like your intuition was speaking to you.

S: If it ever happened, it happened when I was very small, and afterwards, I must have become guarded. I went into my head to filter things rather than through my senses.

C: What comes up for me is the image of a brick wall, between you and your intuition. Is there a possibility that when you think you have an intuitive hunch that some old fear comes up and pushes it away?

TEACHABLE MOMENTS

Fear

The coach's intuition brings up an image of a brick wall as a symbol of the fear that is blocking the client from using their intuition. Fear often masquerades as defensiveness, mental blocks, rationalization, and paralysis by analysis. *Try simply noticing fear and where you feel it in your body (e.g., tense neck, knotted gut, racing heartbeat). When are you afraid to trust your gut instincts? What would it take to feel the fear and do it anyway?*

Aha! Moments

Have you ever noticed how sometimes a "light bulb" goes off in your head, or you get a flash of insight and you suddenly just get it? You *know* - as if you've just remembered something you've always known? That's what we call aha! moments, and they are the key to connecting with our intuition. Aha! moments can show up as a sudden release of tension, a deep sense of calm, a surge of positive energy, a creative jolt, or a powerful feeling that you know what you've got to do. *What aha! has shown up for you recently? How did it show up?*

S: Yes, this may go back forty years, when I withdrew into my head.

C: Did something happen - you don't have to tell me what - to halt your response to intuition?

S: Well, yes, my father died when I was a young boy, and I surrounded myself with some kind of defense...wall... as you suggested.

C: Is there a possibility that when you have an intuitive hit that the old fear comes up and pushes away your wanting to use it?

S: I guess so, because I got so used to not trusting what happens in the moment.

C: I'm wondering what it is about intuition that makes you want to have more of it?

S: A good question. My wife and daughter are very intuitive and notice so many things that I miss. We can be in the same room and we'll notice the same people, but my family picks up certain vibes about the people that I don't get.

C: OK, so if I'm hearing you right, you want to develop your intuition so you can pick up on subtleties. Have you noticed any coincidences lately?

S: Yes, one occurred last week at an interview. I was asked if I could teach a course on listening skills, which I'd never even thought about doing. That night a friend, without knowing anything about this, sent me an e-mail of a listening chart. It may or may not be a coincidence.

C: Let's assume for a moment that this was a meaningful coincidence. Some people call that synchronicity. What might it mean that you ran into two pieces of information in one day about listening skills?

S: Oh, I get it! First an opportunity presented itself, then an answer that this might be a good path for me to follow. It seemed a bit unusual that, right away, I'd get a piece of work that could help me.

C: Great! You just made a quantum leap in your thinking. Intuition is all about this kind of awareness. You'll notice

TEACHABLE MOMENTS

Synchronicity

Often called meaningful coincidences or luck, synchronicity is a compelling sign of intuition in action. Watch for those "chance" occasions where things "just" fall into place; where an answer or opportunity just so happens to present itself soon after you've observed a problem, or where two things happen simultaneously. Synchronicity is a sign of being on a roll, of being in the flow. Your intuition is talking to you, and you're listening by being aware. Synchronicity is always there. It's simply a matter of noticing. *Challenge yourself to notice three synchronistic or coincidental things that happen this week.*

some little thing and then the physical sensation of aha! in your body will happen.

S: A green light so to speak. Well, it did get my attention.

C: Since you are open to this quality of discovery, would you be willing to play a little game like connect the dots? When you notice coincidences, connect one idea with the other. Add up the connections until you see a pattern or a picture emerging. As you become more attuned to the meaning you get, you'll recognize that this is a piece of your own intuition coming back at you.

S: Yes, something like a spool of thread could remind me how all the lines are connected.

C: Good idea! Here's another way to practice. Look at a painting, a magazine cover, a book title, a TV ad, or a tree outside your window, and notice the first word that comes to your mind. Jot down in a little notebook what comes out of the blue.

S: Actually someone just gave me a pocket size notebook yesterday. Aha! Now there's a coincidence! She asked me to write down sudden thoughts that take me by surprise.

C: Good. You told me earlier that you usually live in your head; what can you do to get out of your head? Could you pay attention to somewhere in your body where you feel a reaction?

S: Sometimes I recall a melody when I least expect to, or the way words are said causes a physical reaction; it's something that brings a smile to my face, a feeling beyond words.

C: How might you experience this even more, as a way to help you get in touch with other parts of your body?

S: Well, after listening to the melody, I could see if it relates to some question that's been on my mind.

C: Yes, and allow the melody to enter your body. Feel it in the deepest part of your being, then write down what comes to you. You may be surprised to find that the answer to your question was inside you all along.

TEACHABLE MOMENTS

Intuition's Language

Symbols are the universal language intuition uses to speak to us. They may be symbols from music, art, the workplace, people you know, hobbies; almost anything can serve as a symbol. When you think of "car", what does it represent to you? Money, status, repairs? What kinds of associations come to mind when you hear "love"? Heart, ache, baby, self, Valentine's Day? These are all symbols of the word itself. *Take a moment to stand before a window. What's the first thing you see, hear, or smell? What's that a symbol of; what does it represent to you? What can that association tell you about a problem that's bothering you? Notice any aha! moments that show up.*

S: Yes, I'd like to experience this in as many ways as I can.

C: If intuition speaks mostly through symbols, can you think of some ways you experience life that isn't through words or melodies?

S: Certain shapes capture my imagination, the way someone puts clothes together, or constructs a painting, or the way a flower looks, even the gait of a cat, the way it moves so gracefully.

C: You certainly have heightened sensibilities to be so aware of shapes, colors, and movements. How might this serve your intuition?

S: Well, maybe this kind of attention to detail will guide me in recording impressions and then connecting them through intuition, like we were talking about earlier. Hmm, maybe I'm starting to understand how to get at intuition!

C: Brilliant! What are you willing to do to expand your intuition?

S: I intend to record my impressions and connect my dots, so to speak. I'd also like to try using intuition to help me with my decisions.

C: Looks like your walls are beginning to crumble, don't you think?

S: Yes, I think you've helped me unblock some of that fear.

C: You are farther along on this intuition journey than you may realize. My request for you is to try different ways of being with your intuition. Take a look at the difference it makes when you're being playful, curious, open, or courageous.

Symbols

Intuition speaks through symbols. Here's a way to invite your intuition to speak to you. Take three deep, long breaths. Look at the picture below. What thought or image immediately comes to mind? Write it down. What day dreams or tangents does this word take you to? Go there for a few minutes, without judgment. Use this as food for thought. Brainstorm what this could relate to in your professional or personal life. Which one resonates, i.e., gives you an aha! moment or new perspective?

From the series, *"Lost in Transition"* by SANTJES OOMEN

Dear Intuition Doc

Q: I followed my intuition and since it didn't turn out to be right, I don't trust my intuition anymore. What should I do?

A: You don't need to trust or follow intuition. Just treat it as another source of information.

Q: I suspect my intuition is trying to tell me something and I can't figure out what it is. Can you help?

A: Notice what your attention is drawn to and view things metaphorically. Consider your interpretation as information that might help you find answers to questions. Don't worry about missing an important message - anything worthwhile will be repeated.

Q: I have a good idea what intuition is trying to tell me, but suppose I don't want to hear it?

A: Free will is always an option. You can say no to intuitive guidance.

Q: I understand exactly what my intuition is telling me, but I don't follow it because it's not logical. What do you suggest?

A: Own your intuition. Stick up for it as a part of yourself that can recognize and guide you away from things that are harmful and towards what is best for you.

Q: I am highly sensitive to subtle energies, so I pick up on everyone else's stuff. How can I take care of myself?

A: When your sensitivity is too high or you pick up too much, it helps to have comforting structures like regular diet, sleep, work, play, exercise, etc. Remember to set your boundaries— you can say no!

Three intuition exercises:
let go and play!

1. Dreamsicles: Do you love dreamsicles, too? If you do, here's a new way to enjoy a dream and tickle your intuition to take you from stuck to "licking it!":

    *   Think of a night dream you've had that really stands out. (e.g., you are trying to cross a field to go to the amusement park and an unassuming cow suddenly charges at you.)
    *   What part of the dream do you remember most? A character? A feeling? A place? Write it down. (e.g., the angry cow.)
    *   Notice what else is coming up. What does it make you think of? Quickly write down as many associations that you can think of. The more far-fetched, the better! (e.g., milk, grass, ice cream, bull, Vermont, aliens, death, escape, singing.)
    *   Look at the list and choose the word(s) that jumps off the page at you. Don't think. Just choose. Now! (OK, singing). Wasn't that easy? Intuitive decisions are fun and easy.
    *   Now you get to use your powerful left brain. Analyze, analyze, analyze! How does the word relate to your biggest problem? (e.g., how to stop procrastinating about paperwork.) If you could become that word you chose (pretend, pretend), how would you solve your problem? (e.g., if you became "singing" - *obbh*! - what song is popping into your head right now? e.g., "You, you're making me crazy!") How would you, the song and these words, handle this problem? (e.g., look at the ways procrastination is making me crazy. Then ask what song could take you out of this crazy place. "It's my party and I can cry if I want to". Hmm, what does that say to you? Maybe you need to look at what your choices are doing to you. Is there some rebellious streak that wants to be heard?) Trust your inner

knowing. It will take you where you can be most effectively you.

- Take one action step, no matter how ridiculous it feels to your logical self. One step that this process has suggested. (e.g., choose to say NO to something you "should" do and absolutely don't want to do.) Just do it. See what happens as a result. You may be surprised!

2. Walking Questions: Have you ever noticed how taking a walk *away* from something can bring you back to a new place? Here's a way to let intuition take you to a new level of awareness about something that's on your mind:

- Think of a problem or challenge you're having right now. Make it into a question. Write it down or say it out loud to yourself. (e.g., How can I make more money this year?)
- Leave your surroundings and take a short walk or drive somewhere that's pleasurable for you. It may be in nature, or to a favorite shop, or even across the bridge. The only requirements are that it must be something you enjoy, you must immerse yourself in the experience with as many senses as possible AND you can't think at all about the question/problem while you're gone.
- When you return, ask the question again. (e.g., How can I make more money?) Take five minutes and write down everything that pops into your mind. Don't judge or censure it. Brainstorm as many possibilities as you can. (e.g., spend less, spend more, let people who are "spheres of influence" know what I do, charge more, make that scary call to Deborah to offer a sample session and demonstrate my product, "claim" one person/month that I really want to have as my client, give away more money to my favorite causes, take that vacation I've been dreaming of.)
- Close your eyes and be quiet a moment, listening to your breath.

- When you open your eyes, what idea comes to mind? (e.g., make that scary call to Deborah to offer a sample session and demonstrate my product.)
- Try it.

3. Puzzling Patterns: What's puzzling you? Have you noticed a pattern that keeps repeating itself? Maybe your e-mail program keeps crashing, or you keep losing your wallet. Here's a way to get the message your intuition is trying to send you, so the patterns won't be necessary anymore:

- What's the pattern? Pick something that seems kind of odd; maybe it's happened two or three times in the past few weeks, when it normally doesn't happen. There may be a logical reason for it. Just don't go there right now. Let's see what wisdom your intuition has first! (e.g., you've lost your wallet three times in the last month - something that rarely happens.)
- Ask what the object in the pattern represents. (e.g., wallet = identification and money.)
- Ask yourself how the pattern may be symbolizing something in your life. (e.g., How am I losing my identity? How am I losing money?)
- Work with the question until your gut tells you you're on to something. (e.g., I'm losing my identity by saying yes to stuff I really don't want to do; I'm losing money by spending too much on salaries right now.)
- Take one step to change the pattern. (e.g., say No to something that's draining your energy; hire a temporary employee rather than putting him on payroll.)
- Notice what happens to the pattern as a result. Does it end? If so, your intuition has been heard. If not, play with other options and other steps to take action on the meaning behind the pattern.

How do you tap into your intuition?

Maybe it is merely a matter of asking the first question that comes to your mind, and then noticing what thoughts, feelings, sensations, or observations come up for you. If something clicks, then go with that insight. The key is to keep asking yourself the questions until you reach the Aha! moment.

You are using your intuition today just like you use your other senses of sight, sound, smell, touch, and taste. Intuition is your sixth sense.

Listen to your intuition.

Partner with it.

Experience more synchronicities, more coincidences.

Discover a sense of curiosity, enthusiasm, and adventure.

Connect with the chaos around you.

Move with the speed of change AND join us as we leap into the new millennium –
THE AGE OF INTUITION. (Drum roll, please!)

What good are road maps in the country of the blind?"

The journeys I take to wherever it is I am going
rarely seem to be the ones I choose.
And if there is a third eye to inform me,
an eye of the mind, that too can be guided
like a brush steered with the hand.

Excerpt from "Lost in Transition" by Santjes Oomen

The Intuition Collaborative
'KNOW THY SELF'

Imagine making a Quantum Leap in Intuition

The Coaches of the Intuition Collaborative specialize in co-creating breakthroughs in love, service, and inspired leadership for amazing individuals and organizations. The Intuition Collaborative's professional services include personalized one-to-one and group coaching, dialogue circles, workshops, and training programs that are powerful and fun catalysts for deep learning, conscious communication, and collaborative action.

The Promises of Intuition Coaching

- You will acquire the know-how to translate subtle intuitive impressions into practical and effective guidance you can use in real life situations.
- You will gain an empowering new perspective about fear and desire that sets you free to choose new possibilities for yourself and the world.
- You will establish personal standards and boundaries that honor your intuition and provide the foundation for living an extraordinary life.
- You will develop powerful listening skills that deepen your ability to love and be loved by others.
- You will trust that your intuition is a valuable source of inspiration and discovery.

About the Intuition Collaborative:
Jeannine Ayres, Morgaine Beck, Suzee Ebeling, Sharon Hooper, and Lauren Lee

Jeannine Ayres, a personal coach, founded "At The Water's Edge, Center for Intuitive Living" where she inspires individuals and groups to reconnect their inner spirit with nature, in order to simplify their lives and reduce stress. She has an M.A. in Communications, is a public speaker, a part-time college professor, and author of "*50 Tips to Achieve Harmony and Balance*".

Morgaine Beck is a life coach who integrates her background in communications training and fulfillment consulting with co-creating extraordinary lives for her clients. She works with people who want a jump-start partner to move them, under their own power, to full speed ahead. Morgaine is known for her ingenious intuition, sizzling synchronicity, powerful personality process, soul support, and "get real" roots.

Suzee Ebeling, a mentor coach, delights in helping clients use their intuition to bring greater love and deeper wisdom into their lives. She is founder of the Center for Intuitive Learning at IntuitionCoach.com, and a faculty member of two professional coach training organizations. Suzee presented her vision for the future of Intuition Coaching at the ICF 2000 Conference in Vancouver.

Sharon Hooper is a business coach specializing in creativity and product development. Her successful background as an entrepreneur has led to national awards, and her workshops have influenced hundreds of people to create their own infinite magic. Sharon has a passionate desire to inspire others to attain their highest goals through vision, intuition, courage, and focus.

Lauren Lee is a personal coach who partners with intelligent, successful people who want to excel at their careers and their lives by expressing their passions, their gifts, and their unique talents in a way that brings them success, happiness, money, and balance. Lauren's 15+ years in the fast-paced, high-tech computer software industry have given her a track record of success and first-hand experience to understand the challenges faced in creating a fulfilling life blending spirituality into the workplace. She is passionately dedicated to her clients' success! Lauren also cultivates an on-line women's community (www.womensu.com) for women to connect, learn, grow, and prosper.

Contact us for a free sample session and ways to bring intuition alive in your organization:

coaches@intuitioncollaborative.com

(941) 659-2685

Mirnda will be back
on Dec 23/04

Jessie - Supervisor
_____

7:30-3 pm
Daycare Centre

Trinity Baptist -
(604) 264-1192

Dec. 231 - Thursday